May this book
you and encourage you o
your journey! May the love
of God fill your heart as you
live a high-powered life in the
Lord. Greater awaits!
Go forth w/ power!

blessings,

Michelle L. Primeil
2022

The High-Powered
Woman

Michelle L. Primeaux

For more information, contact: Michelle Primeaux
www.michellelprimeaux.com
Cover photo by Wayne Shot It Visuals, LLC
The High-Powered Woman Logo by Sophistique Graphics.

The High-Powered Woman
September 2021
Published by Pink Butterfly Press LLC
www.PinkButterflyPressllc.com
Paperback/Ebook/Hardcover
Pink Butterfly Press LLC

This book is in honor of my Daddy, the late Elder Levert C. Todd, the first man ever to love me. He purchased my first typewriter. Most importantly, he introduced me to Jesus Christ.

Although my father passed away 21 years ago, I still feel his love, and I smile at the unforgettable memories.

I remember all the beautiful things he taught me.

Daddy made a significant impact on my life and was one of the most incredible and brilliant men I will ever know.
I love you, Daddy.

Your baby girl for life,

Michelle -AKA- Shellfish

Acknowledgments

I give glory and honor to you, God, for your Grace and Mercy that never left me and your love that saved me. Thank you for leading me to a place of abundance in you. I love you, Lord, with everything in me. It is in you that I live, move, and have my being.

To my amazing husband, Brandon Hassan Primeaux, you are God's golden gift to me. I am grateful for how you love me with everything you have. You are my love, best friend, minister, covering, and my life partner. I appreciate every sacrifice you made to help me birth the vision. Thank you for believing in me. You are proof of God's redemptive love in my life. I love you, my Caramel King. Team Primeaux for life!

To my firstborn, Dwayne A Johnson, Jr., who has been with me for more than half of my life, I had no clue how to be a mother at 17. But, God gave us everything we needed to grow up together. You were so easy to love. You have been an amazing son, and I love watching you raise your son. I am so proud of the man you have become. You are the best photography artist around. Thank you for encouraging me to reach for the stars. Continue to live on purpose, son, and remember that faith without works is dead. I love you, mighty man of valor!

To A'zhana M. Ford, my Baby-Kakes, I prayed to God for a daughter, and when the doctor said, "it's a girl," my heart leaped for joy. I promised God I would love you and take care of you. You taught me how to be courageous. I have watched you continue to show up no matter what. I am so proud of all your accomplishments and excited to see you earn your BS degree in 2022. Thank you for being a listening ear during this process. You are so beautiful. Remember that without faith, it is impossible to please God. I love you so much, baby girl! Mighty woman of valor!

To my phenomenal bonus children, Titus, Seth, and Brandy – The Primeauxs; you came into my life and my heart just melted. Your love and support have meant so much to me. You are all a gift from God. I am so blessed to know you, grow with you, and love you. Thank you for choosing to love me. I cherish the extraordinary and priceless times we have together. Always stay together no matter what. Be bold and keep God first. Remember, you can do all things through Christ, who gives you strength. I love you, precious Primeauxs! Mighty men and woman of valor! Rest in Heaven Samuel U. Primeaux, our hearts miss you tremendously. You continue to be my inspiration.

I am a fabulous Gigi because of my super awesome Grandson, Kendrick O. Johnson. You are my pride and joy, young man, and the smartest, coolest, and most loving grandson. I'm looking forward to reading your first book. God's hand is upon you, and you will do mighty things in your lifetime. Always dream big and make your dreams a reality. Always put God first and say your prayers. I love you, Grandson! You are my sunshine forever!

To my Queen Mommy, Sandra L. Todd. I have so many reasons why I love you and so many memories too numerous to recount. The memory that replays the most is when I called you and asked if I could come home. You so gently said, "yes." I can't thank God enough for choosing me to be born from your womb. I am the woman I am today because of you. You never gave up on me. You lift me when I'm down, pray for me when I am weak, and sing to me when I'm sad. You are always there for me, and you never stopped loving me. You are my cheerleader, mentor, teacher, nurturer, and best friend. I love you, Mommy. You are my Queen always.

Grandma Louise D. Deligar, I am intrigued by your tenacity and strength. Your love for God has stood the test of time. You are an example of class, beauty, and wisdom. I will cherish your prayers, advice, virtue, and love for a lifetime. I pray that I can continue in the rich legacy of spiritual royalty and faithfulness to God for the next generation. I love you so much.

We are the Todds for life! To my siblings, Patrice, Levette, Levert Jr., and Lamarr. The fond memories we have and the new memories we create together keep me smiling during rough times. The Todd household goes down in history as the best. Thank you for your support, encouragement, advice, bailouts, and unconditional love. You guys know me best. Continue to impact the lives of others. You all inspire me. I know Daddy would be so proud of each of you. I love you, family to life.

To my Mom and Dad in love, Paul and Karen Primeaux-Smith, you guys have been spectacular in my life. Thank you for loving me as your daughter, sacrificing for our family, and being a tremendous support. Momma, our special moments of fire during prayer and your encouragement are priceless. I love you both to life. Dad, I am ready for our crab date.

My best friend forever, Sheri L. Bruton-Shavers. For over 40 years, we have been best friends. You are more than a friend; you are my beautiful sister. The support over the years has been genuine and unforgettable. We have gone from diapers to ministry together for the Lord, and I could not have asked for a better BFF. Thank you for being there in the good and bad, spoiling me, and never giving up on a Sista. I love you always, best friend.

Minister Georgette Peterson and Angela Brooks, you ladies were God-sent. You saw the best in me and have been mentors, my confidantes, and most of all, honest, generous, and loving friends. You both helped to empower me to greatness. I will always be grateful for our friendship. Now it's time for our weekend getaway. Love you so much, my Sisters!

To the very phenomenal women of Love and Faith Ministries, I thank you for your remarkable contributions to my life over the last seven years. I have grown into a better woman, minister, and Bible teacher. Your love has been overwhelming, your support incredible, and your love for God inspires me. You ladies have extraordinary stories, and together, we win! Continue to unite in love, my sisters. The best is yet to come! I love you, my sisters in the faith, and my friends.

To my lovely Pastor, Florence Freeman of The Temple of Prayer Church, Inc, in Chester, Pennsylvania. You were God-sent indeed. You are full of wisdom. I am grateful that you saw the anointing in my life and encouraged me in a special way that inspired me to go higher and grow in ministry and the Lord. I thank God for your leadership and genuine love and support to my family and me. I love you, Pastor. May God continue to use you to raise up leaders with power and truth.

Dr. Nephetina Serrano, your life is indeed a ministry of empowerment. God connected us, and I am ever more inspired to be bold and move out strong. It's an honor to call you, friend. I love you, my Sister.

Table of Contents

Forward

I feel both sincerely grateful and immensely privileged to have the honor of commenting on this beautiful piece of work. It celebrates the beauty in and of womanhood. The word *beauty* is often used to reference women. This book celebrates the inner and external beauty of women. It defines the High-Powered Woman as the "salt of the Earth," which is true. Women are the salt of the Earth. Their in-built generosity of spirit and in-born emotional intelligence enhances the flavor of our existence through a genuine sensitivity to the needs of others.

"The High-Powered Woman" easily qualifies as one of the most remarkable books I have ever read. I have read many books and even co-authored one with my loving husband. Not to mention, I've contributed content to many other works. However, this author's rendering is incredibly engaging to me. I think that you, the reader, will share in that sentiment.

Michelle Primeaux describes the High-Powered Woman with a simplicity that we all can understand. It is refreshing to discover that the High-Powered Woman is not necessarily the bronzed beauty living in a ten-room mansion, who's wearing only Prada and Coco Chanel, driving a Ferrari, and making regular jet-sets to the South of France on her vacations. The author empowers our confidence by informing us that each of us is a High-Powered Woman, from the lady handing out fast food at a Wendy's drive-thru to that bronzed beauty living in the ten-room mansion. They both are High-Powered women — along with every other woman in-between.

The author's language exudes *f*aith, love, and hope. Ultimately, she speaks the language of absolute trust. The trust we need to continue to abide in the eternal loving wisdom of God. The author expresses herself with clarity of thought. While reading this book, I continually received the impression that I was reading the thoughts of a pure mind. I realized that although she had been through past trauma, she sought comfort and rest in the healing power and the special grace of God, which is present in His unfailing and unconditional love.

This book's entrance into the literary market is quite timely. I am particularly excited about its title, The High-Powered Woman. When the author requested that I write this forward, it left me only too honored and happy to oblige.

Michelle Primeaux successfully presented us with a picture of a High-Powered Woman who now crosses her world with faith, confidence, purpose, and grace. Even if a High-Powered Woman's spirit is restless, within the pages of this beautiful book, she could find the strength to quietly and firmly utter her truth without doubt or hesitation. She would be free to lead a life submerged in the abiding grace of God.

Thank you, Michelle, for reminding us that we are queens over our dominions, worthy of the glittering dividends of a life well-lived. And that is why, after reading this book, we should be able to step out with confidence and faith in our worthiness to receive the very best that life has to offer.

Thank you, and God bless,
Dr. Nephetina L. Serrano

Relationship Expert, "The Marriage CEO"
Co-Founder/ CEO *Covenant Marriages, Covenant Rescue 911, Covenant Marriages Institute, Philadelphia, Pennsylvania.*

Dr. Nephetina L. Serrano is an Evangelist, International Inspirational Speaker, Award-winning #1 International Best-Selling Author, 3xs Amazon Best Seller, Co-Host T.V. Show "Your Marriage Matters," Publisher Marriage CEO Magazine, Owner, Serrano Legacy Publishing Co., Award Winner 100 Best Coaches "Success Magazine 2021

All social media: *www.MarriageCEOs360.com*
Email: *www.DrSerranoministries@gmail.com*

The High-Powered Woman

Introduction

I am not a millionaire! I do not live in a mansion! I do not drive a luxury car! I do not fly by private jet to the South of France for weekend shopping trips. I am not a household name. The truth is, outside of my husband, I might not be described as a high-powered woman. Yet, I *am* a high-powered woman! I overcame intense experiences in life, survived abuse, healed from my past, blasted through barriers, and most importantly, entered into a grand relationship with the creator of all things, the mighty and wise God of the universe, and the Lord of my life. I became a new woman in Jesus Christ and my value and worth increased. My life is considered priceless, and it is progressively advancing. I am a woman with the Power of God, a purpose, and a Plan.

When people think of high-powered women, they might think of Forbes Magazine's Top 100 Women of the Year. The list includes high-profile CEOs, famous entertainers, or very wealthy individuals. Over the years, we have seen their faces come across our television screens, their stories have graced the pages of countless magazines, we've read about them in books and admired their accomplishments and status from afar.

However, through my spiritual journey, I have discovered that the true meaning of a high-powered woman is much more than what society deems it. It's not the top, the best, or even the most remarkable woman. The high-powered woman can be any woman, from a food service worker to a CEO. It doesn't matter what she does; all that matters is that she does it well and continues to elevate in life.

The high-powered woman is you, and she is me; there are no color barriers, no income restrictions, and no educational requirements. High-powered women are everywhere, from suburban yacht clubs to the urban community center. They are on the busy streets of New York City and the plateaus of Asia. They are beyond the sea in Jamaica, and living in the Alaskan mountains. High-powered women are strategically placed throughout the nations and AMAZING in their own right by the power of God and their choice to live!

Throughout the history of time, many women have gone through too much even to tell it all. We have endured and overcome the impossible. And still, we rise from heaps and heaps of ashes from the pits of life. I am intrigued by women's spirits. I believe every woman has within her so much more than she even recognizes. God created a beautiful masterpiece in you. You possess so many shining facets exuding light from your soul, illuminating where you stand. Every woman has the potential and capability to be a powerful force as God willed. Our journeys are all different, and we have seen the worst of life, yet we are still here. We have been abandoned, rejected, criticized, doubted, overlooked, attacked, hated, confused, broken, hurt, ashamed, guilty, abused, fearful, and handicapped. But, I see more Queens emerging. I see great courage, tenacity, and strong faith that was always inside of them. I know the overcomer status. The impoverished I see becoming wealthy. The most educated and influential women I see elevating even higher. What stands out like a beautiful picture is God's grace upon your life and the activation of His power within you. There is a high-powered woman in you.

On my journey to understanding life and my purpose in it, I found God. I discovered in the Holy Bible every answer to my life's issues and concerns. I was drawn to the scriptures, specifically the stories of the different women. I saw myself and others in their stories, and I was intrigued to study and go deeper into what God was teaching me about me through these women.

For the past ten years of studying the bible, with seven of those years teaching women, I have discovered the truth and unique things about life and how to live life abundantly. But, it wasn't until I read the entire Bible that I drew closer to him and divinely experienced His power. I saw His power that was so intensely illuminated throughout the scriptures and reflected on His power that had been a driving force in my life even when I didn't recognize it.

Webster defines the phrase high-powered as a very successful, important, and powerful person. While this is very true, society has a different standard in declaring success, which is essential, and by what means, they are powerful. The scripture says in 1 *Samuel 16:7* – "…*The Lord does not look at the things people see. People look at the outward appearance, but the Lord looks at the heart.*" The power we have is from God, and we sure do need it in this world we live in. We cannot do it alone. *Ephesians 3:20 - "Now to him who can do exceedingly abundantly above all that we ask or think, according to the power that works within us. "*

After reading this book, you will experience what a high-powered woman looks like and what it takes to be a high-powered woman from a biblical perspective. May you be unveiled as the shining gem and very precious woman that you are. Take a journey with me as you become inspired, empowered, have greater confidence and an even greater drive to fulfill your God-given purpose with power. You will be leaping in your soul and not afraid to proclaim that you are a high-powered woman. Additionally, you will walk away with confidence and more faith in the power of the Holy Spirit that dwells in the life of every believer of Jesus Christ.

We can do greater than what we have ever imagined and go beyond the limits of our thinking to become the high-powered women God has purposed and called us to be.

Chapter 1
A High-Powered Savior

The day my father died was the most devastating and horrific day of my life. It was apparent that my life was over. How could I ever live without my daddy? My father had a unique charm that always made me feel superior in his presence. From my perspective, he was the best father and person in the world; he was the epitome of what a human being should be. Levert Todd, Sr., age 55, left this earth way too soon but left many memories to last a lifetime. After twenty-one years since his passing, I continue to remember him, smile, and sometimes even cry.

Who could describe a man of such great character and grand influence? My father impacted the lives of everyone he connected with. He was a very handsome man who stood tall at six foot three, medium build, with a caramel brown complexion and black hair. I would often position myself on my tippy toes to see how tall I could be next to this giant. His gregarious and contagious smile lit up the room and drew people in effortlessly. My father displayed joy, and one could always hear him whistling and singing throughout the house and as he strolled down the city blocks. The personality he portrayed was warm, gentle, loving, comforting, and very funny. He was brilliant and amazed me with his use of words. God gifted my father with wisdom and knowledge; he seemed always to know what to say and do.

Growing up, I intently watched my father's interaction with others. It was beautiful to see him treat all people the same, whether the owner at the corner store, the bus driver or the homeless man he passed every day on his way to work or church. I was intrigued at how my father could talk to anyone without even knowing them. I watched his smile, his hand motions as he spoke, and the involved expression he always had when speaking to others. He instilled a strong sense of value in his children and the people he communicated with. My father was a local preacher in the city and received rapturous applause after each sermon. He knew almost everyone, and they knew him. You would often find him studying the bible, dictionary, yes, the dictionary, and even the encyclopedia, of which he owned two sets. You would also find him studying medical books and anything to do with fish and animals. Life with my father was incredible from my perspective, so that is why it was extremely devastating to hear of him being rushed to the hospital.

While at home, in the middle of a cold December afternoon, I received a telephone call from my eldest sister informing me that my father was taken to the hospital. I began to panic, and so many thoughts flooded my head. I immediately got dressed. I had not fully recovered from my cesarean delivery only two weeks prior, yet I was determined to learn what happened to my father. As I entered the room in the hospital's emergency section, I was disturbed to see several tubes coming from his body. There was no one else in the room except for the nurse. I explained to her who I was, and she informed me that my mother and eldest sister had just left to go to the cafeteria and that my father was not entirely coherent and probably would not know who I was because he did not know who my mother and sister were before I arrived. As she continued to speak, he awakened softly and said the words that still bring tears to my eyes this day, "Baby Girl." I smiled and went over to his bedside and began to tell him how much I loved him as tears flowed down my face, not knowing that this would be the last time that I would ever be able to see my father alert, responsive, and call me "Baby Girl."

When my mother and sister arrived back to the room, my father was more coherent, and we talked with him and even teased him when suddenly, his body began to seize. It was frightening to watch my father's body jerk uncontrollably, while the doctors insisted that we leave the room. This was the beginning of the end for my father. My dear father's health took a turn for the worse. The information that the doctor gave to my family was hard to embrace, in fact, I do not believe any of us could truly embrace the inevitable. With the doctors standing in front of us with information about my father, my mind was tormented with thoughts of living without my father. Not my father, the only father I would ever know. This could not be happening. Well, it was happening at that very moment. The doctors informed us that it was now just a waiting period. A few days later around 4:00 a.m. while I was sleeping rather restlessly, the telephone rang. I looked at the caller I.D. on my cordless phone, and in my soul, I knew the unbelievable had occurred. My mother, speaking in a calm tone, instructed me to get to the hospital as soon as possible.

My eldest sister picked me up, and when we both arrived at the hospital; mom was there. As we entered dad's room, we immediately saw he had passed away. The breathing machine, heart monitors, and other tubes were disconnected from my father's lifeless body. I looked toward the window with the idea to somehow break it and jump, while my eldest sister just fell to the floor in devastation. My mother remained calm through it all. This was a day of despair, not knowing that life goes on, and in time, I could live without the presence of my father here on earth with us. It has been 21 years since my father's death, and I still love and miss him. As a parent, I instill in my children all the things I learned from my father and his legacy lives on. My father's living was not in vain and his assignment here on earth was full and complete. He is at rest, and that leaves me with an abundance of comforting peace that passes all understanding. Although, immediately after my father died, I did not see nor understand any of what I know today. Initially, my emotions were too overwhelming to handle. I had so many questions with feelings of anger, hurt, sadness, sorrow, and much grief. My daddy, the one who picked me up from elementary school each day, the one who made up songs about me, who put me on his shoulders as he walked to the store, and the one who I looked to as my savior. My daddy, who had an answer for everything and the one who I never imagined would leave me, was gone forever. Where is my savior now? Who would save me? I needed a savior because I was lost and had been for a long time.

Every high-powered woman has a story. Each of our stories has a beginning, a middle, and an end! Although we cannot control everything about our stories, we can make decisions that impact our lives each time we experience a new day of living. It has taken me many years to begin to understand certain aspects of life, such as gains, losses, suffering, overcoming obstacles, enduring grief, and knowing joy. But oftentimes, before the high-powered woman truly emerges, she has endured life's hardships. She is often broken, tired, confused, hurt, and most likely believes she can no longer endure this life. Perhaps she believes she lost herself, has no purpose, or wants desperately for the hurt and pain to end. This woman could possibly feel alone, without hope, and desperately needing to be rescued.

Who does not want to be rescued? Rescued from danger. Rescued from disaster. Rescued from a bad relationship. Rescued from poverty. Rescued from a dreaded job. How about just being rescued from one's own self and uncontrollable thoughts and behaviors. Whatever it is, there seems to always be a need to be rescued.

As a little girl I loved fairy tale movies that always revealed at the end a beautiful young girl being rescued by a great and handsome Prince. As a teenager, I loved romantic movies that told stories of everyday ordinary women being pursued by wealthy men and given the grandest luxuries of life. I would imagine myself in those roles and tremendously desired it all. As a little girl, teenager, and even throughout adulthood, I have always admired the way love was portrayed. The charming ways in which it was acted out in the movies was extraordinary and simply a dream to me.

As I would think about my poor life, I would veer off into deep thoughts, imagine a man falling in love with me, rescuing me, and carrying me off into a rich world of eternal happiness. Other than the love my parents displayed, I had never witnessed it except on television, so the likelihood of it happening for me was very slim. However, it sure did not stop me from dreaming. I believed my father was my savior for so long; however, I also wanted the fairy-tale life that portrayed another kind of savior. I know that I am not alone on this one. Over the years, I have had countless conversations with women who dreamt of being rescued by prince charming, and some still do.

My best friend and I had fantasies about marrying a rich man who would buy us a huge house with a white picket fence. We decided that we would have two beautiful children, a boy and a girl, to make our family complete. They would be cared for with no worries because our husbands would make sure we had everything we needed. For some, they may have outgrown their childhood fantasies of the princess and the frog, the beauty and beast, and the lady and the tramp, but not me. The desire to be saved was real. The need for a savior applies to all breathing, blood pumping, and thinking minds of humankind. The truth is we were created with an indwelling desire to be loved and rescued; therefore, we seek it, are drawn to it, imagine it, and even pray for it. As we continue our journey in life, we will eventually realize…we need a Savior!!!

Reflection is powerful when it can reveal what is lying deep in the soul! As I mentioned earlier, I was lost for a long time. As far as I can remember, I felt ruined, rejected, worthless, and lonely. I felt ruined by the color of my skin, my struggle with reading comprehension, my buck teeth, and my embarrassing lisp. In addition, I was fearful and shy, lacking confidence in who I was or what I did. It is a terrible misfortune for a person to feel deeply discouraged and gloomy, especially at such a young age. When I think about the word ruin, I think damaged. I felt that somehow God intentionally messed up when he created me. Those thoughts led to impoverished thinking, frustration, feelings of being a failure, and a complete disaster. As often as I reflected on my feelings about looks, intellect, and capabilities, I felt so dejected and unsettled. The painful and ugly truth of how I viewed myself was hidden for many years. Unfortunately, my behavior spoke much louder than the voice in my head. It screamed "help!" "I'm ruined." "Somebody, save me." The question is "was I truly ruined?"

Ruined

The word ruin is defined as the state of being ruined; the remains of something destroyed; a ruined building, person, or object, according to Merriam Webster's Dictionary. The word ruined as a verb is to damage irreparably; bankrupt, impoverish; to subject to frustration, failure, or disaster; to reduce to ruins, to devastate. So, the answer to my question "was I ruined?" Maybe not in a physical sense, but my catastrophic thinking, perception, and emotions led to low moods and manifested behaviors that were ruining my character, sense of self-worth, and self-esteem. I believed my reputation was being ruined because of my treacherous acts of betrayal. I became spiritually impoverished and bankrupt.

What causes something to be ruined? Once upon a time it was intact, beautiful, and useful. Perhaps, due to decay, mishandling, lack of care and maintenance, that beautiful something may become ruined. Even natural disasters, intentional acts of destruction, and battles have been a factor in a structure becoming dilapidated. All around the world we see ruins in cars, homes, buildings, and even towns. In fact, there are famous ruins all around the world from ancient sites of Rome, Egypt, and China. Once I visited Fort Charlotte in Nassau, Bahamas that was built in 1789. This historical place is still standing but looks worn down and only used for tourism.

As I travel from city to city, I see the remains of homes ruined by fire or neglect. What was once thriving areas with booming businesses are now empty shells. Where there were beautifully landscaped homes that flowed from one end of the city and held together strong families are now dilapidated and covered with graffiti. Cities that once represented community and strength, are now a breeding ground for strongholds, vacant lots of empty dreams, and dark allies of hope deferred. Even the great number of schools we once learned in are closed or torn down and replaced by prison facilities. It makes you pause and pose the question... What happened?

If you ponder what the word ruin really means, it is disturbing, especially when I connected it to what was going on in my life. I was not alone, the silent cries of so many have been overlooked for so long. Many are decaying inside just as I did, year after year, not saying a mumbling word to anyone. I had a strong ability to mask my deepest and greatest fears and pain. Just as I mentioned cars, homes, buildings, cities, and ancient sites that are ruined due to neglect, battles, and natural disasters, the same is happening to many areas of people's lives. However, what constitutes damage will differ from person to person based upon their perception. Whether it is an unexpected health crisis, rejection and or abandonment from loved ones, or financial collapse that can easily throw someone into a state of feeling ruined. Or perhaps it was a result of abuse, homelessness, weariness from fighting for freedom and equal rights or divorce. Well, to answer the question…yes, I was ruined. I had collapsed spiritually, mentally, morally, physically, economically, and socially. In my mind, I was simply the remains of something destroyed. This left me completely lost.

A Lost Bewildered Soul

What I had hoped for could never be. I hoped I could have turned back time and made better decisions in life. I wished my father would come back, my looks would change for the better, my world perfect, and my reason for living explained. No one told me that life was this hard and why am I the only person who is miserable? How is everyone around me happy? They have no idea how bad I am hurting and how bad I no longer have a desire to live. Even my children are better off without me, a worthless life with no direction, no purpose, and one who constantly fails. At this point in my life, my thoughts had consumed me, and it felt as though my faith had run away with hope, leaving me lost and bewildered. I just wanted to die! This was after many years of dealing with tormenting thoughts!

One evening, as I sat on the edge of my bed with my bedroom door closed and my children in their beds, I silently wept and wept and wept for what seemed like hours. The pain within was so forceful, and I could not take the pressure that weighed so heavily on my chest that felt as though someone with great strength was pressing down on my heart and lungs until I could hardly breathe. That rooted pain from feelings of hopelessness, helplessness, loneliness, and purposelessness is what made me want to do more than scream and end every painful thought, memory, possible future disappointments, and heartbreak. I imagined what my life was going to look like in the future, and I wanted no parts. I envisioned a torturous life beyond the perimeter of my four walls and my anxiety heightened. My thoughts that night caused a deeper pain than what I was already experiencing and the thought of my pain never-ending was a pain unexplainable or unbearable. A pain that could not be taken away by another bowl of my favorite Mint Chip ice cream, a trip to the hairdresser, a new pair of fabulous shoes, in the arms of a man, a luxurious vacation, or money in the bank.

This dark feeling was a strong force. I remember the silence in my home that night. Nothing to hear but my chaotic thoughts and the question I repeatedly asked God, Why? Why? Why? I believed that at that present moment, there was no longer a reason to live. I began to write my resignation letter to my children and my family expressing why I was done with life and unable to go any further. I was resigning from life. I wanted to express everything that was in my heart. I finally had the heart to let go of life and people who seemed to constantly defeat me...life had won. But that night, something happened that would change my entire life forever.

With a broken heart, blurry eyes, and tears running down my face like a faucet, I began to walk to the bathroom to take one final look at myself in the mirror before I left my house forever. As I began to walk, right in the middle of my room, a heavy feeling came over me. I fell to the floor in anguish and pain screaming my disdain towards God. I then felt what was like a light sheet cover me and I heard in my spirit, the words "Michelle, I Love you and will never leave you." In an instant, my spirit felt different as if hope had been restored, and I screamed "I WANT TO LIVE!" As I laid there on my knees, I just wept with my face to the floor. I begged God to forgive me for all I had done as I just kept repeating that I was sorry, and I wanted to live.

My cry began to change. This cry was different, it was a cry of joy because I knew I had been rescued. That was the night my High-powered Savior showed up to save me. I was saved from myself and the plan of Satan. The amazing revelation hit me; I had just heard God's voice for the first time, and He called me by my name! That night on my bedroom floor, I was saved not just from committing suicide, but from the strongholds that held me captive for so long as a prisoner in my own mind. There was a divine encounter that occurred and would change the course of my destiny and begin to shape the high-powered woman that I would soon discover.

But there was something that I did not learn until later and that was, I had a choice to believe, surrender my heart and soul, repent, and LIVE! I did just that! My heart desired God and desired to live. I no longer wanted to end my life. The reality is that my circumstances did not change; however, my belief system did, and my hope was restored.

Some may read this and be unable to fully understand how a person could be so low to the point of wanting to end their own life. But mental illness is very real and is sweeping through homes, communities, in the workplace, at the playground, in the schools, and inside the walls of church buildings. The American Foundation for Suicide Prevention reports that suicide is the 10th leading cause of death in the U.S. in 2019 as 47,511 Americans died by suicide. This is alarming to learn about, and that is why each day that I wake up, it is my heart's desire to be God's messenger and fulfill His plan for my life. We never know who is suffering silently and in need of Jesus Christ, the world's Savior. My story is not everyone's story, but it is important to understand that in our human nature, we are not invincible, and at some point, we are capable of breaking. In this life, we need a higher power than us to help us through, and that is the power of the Holy Spirit by way of our faith in Jesus Christ. This is what I believe according to the scriptures. I am a witness to the miraculous work God is able to do in any willing soul.

What was once ruined in my life would be restored and able to be used by God. What had collapsed would be re-established. My mind went through a transformation process and continues to be transformed. Thoughts of destruction were replaced with the truth of the Word of God. I became a new creation according to 2 Corinthians 5:17 and was reborn again according to John 3:3. To be reborn is to be filled with God's Holy Spirit, and to be filled with the Holy Spirit is to believe in Jesus Christ who is declared to be the way to God and eternal life.

"For God so loved the world that he gave his only begotten son, that whosoever believes in him shall not perish but have everlasting life." – John 3:16

Sometimes, we desire a savior because it seems so easy, romantic, and beautiful. The innate desire for a savior was always a place reserved for God, but I filled it with everything but Him. I had to die that night, just to live! It was me saying yes to Christ. That was just the beginning of me becoming a high-powered woman and it was not going to be easy; yet possible! It would be the power of God that would do, "exceedingly abundantly above all I could ask or think according to the power that works in me." – Ephesians 3:20

And today, when I look into the eyes of my husband, my children, and my six-year old grandson, who proudly calls me "Gigi," I give God praise that I am still here. And when I preach, teach, coach, and serve others, gratitude floods my spirit, because I never imagined God using me to impact the lives of others. Guess what? I almost ended my life because of a season of pain and the false belief I surrendered to. God is a healer and the truth!

Today, I am filled with the power of the Holy Spirit and hope. God's redemptive power has been evident upon my life and within my very soul. I am clear about my worth, purpose, the valued warrior inside of me, and so much more. I am so glad I found my Savior, or shall I say, He found me. I said YES and chose LIFE! Come on my sisters, let the high-powered woman emerge!

Chapter 2
A High-Powered Faith

Fully assured in the hope. The choice to live is everything! Some live and some merely exist. Some believe that life cannot get any better, while some look for opportunities to live a productive life. Why we choose to live is important to know within our very souls. Life will produce unpredictable and overwhelming moments that we never expected to experience. These shocking moments in time can last longer than we could have ever anticipated. After some time, you may ask, "What is this all for?"

Faith is a word that is spoken quite often although not always practiced. We often say that we have faith in God; yet, when life's hardships come knocking at our door, we often blame God and believe our lives are ruined. The reality is that we are often shaken by the bitter occurrences that blow into our lives. For some, they become stuck in the storm and cannot see a way out. Some are stuck in the past and are not able to enjoy life and be fulfilled by the daily blessings of God.

Do you remember Lot's wife? In Genesis, God told Lot to take his family and leave the city because He was going to destroy it. He told them to go and not look back. Well, Lot's wife looked back and turned into a pillar of salt. I believe when she looked back, there was a deep longing in her heart for this place that did not have the presence of God there. God was destroying this place because of the wickedness there. He had a new place prepared for her family; however, her heart desired the opposite of what God had for her. She could not see beyond her present and past. She threw away her future because she could not let go and trust God for greater things.

How are you progressing each day in life? Do you find yourself constantly looking back and longing for the days of old? What fuels you to keep living? What is your faith and hope in? What is your reason for enduring the everyday issues of life? Is your reason based upon something temporal or something eternal?

The night I was prepared to end my life was based upon thoughts that were not producing the whole truth and influenced my emotions that included a distorted perception of my reality. My encounter with God empowered me as I died to my old self that night and was ready to embark on a journey that would reveal the power of God in my life. Before my encounter with God, I only saw Him from a limited understanding and perspective; therefore, I was not living according to God's plan and purpose for my life. In fact, I was only existing each day. I did not follow the guidance of my moral compass, lacked wisdom, and had little knowledge of God's character. I never understood that my identity was in God. I did not see any hope and did not think anything new, good, or exciting could spring up from my dead mindset.

I grew impatient, decided to no longer live, and take matters into my own hands. Throughout life, I believed things would just come in an instant, and when they did not happen as I expected them to, I attached defeat and failure to it. I was with the many others in the scriptures and our society today, who thrive on instant gratification. When life doesn't go as we plan, we begin to look for different alternatives that will appease us or release us from the agony of it all. In these times, we are experiencing the fast movement of time, and in keeping up with the fast pace of the world, we oftentimes desire things to be quick, easy, and painless, including death.

When it comes to life, some choose to live, and some choose to die. I was one in the number choosing the latter. The pain and misery that come with this life can cause one to question the point of their continued existence. But to trust God to the very end of our time here on earth will require faith! What could happen if you don't give up?

During research, I learned of the much controversial "Death with Dignity Act." This is a law approved in some states that allow certain patients diagnosed with a terminal illness to end their life early, assisted by a physician. This choice in shortening life is an option gaining popularity. Death; something that was once accepted as a normal part of our human existence is now avoided through the power of convenience.

A person may feel that battling a terminal illness each day of their life diminishes its value, and desire for it to end. The Death with Dignity Act allows for a physician assisted death for a patient who wishes not to live out their terminal illness diagnosis to the very end. With approval of this act, a person receives aid in dying by a physician who prescribes a lethal dose of medication that will deliberately end a person's life. This medication is taken orally by the patient at a designated date and time of their choice. Some medical professionals, political supporters, and segments of society consider this type of death to be dignified as a person should be able to choose to live or die.

However, I believe that when one takes a lethal dose of medicine to end their life prior to their naturally appointed time, is an act of suicide. I too, at a point in my life was no different from those who choose this route until I understood that there was a God who was the creator of humankind and had a plan for each person's life. I also learned that to take my life would be acting as if I am God. His love for me went far beyond life's sufferings and disappointments. Whatever time we are given here in life should be lived on purpose with meaning. Life is precious and hard at the same time. We do not know when our circumstances will change and when our end here on earth will come; however, with understanding, one can take heart and live. My life was a gift, and to choose life would later reveal years of amazing events that God had planned just for me.

The inability to cope with life's circumstances and the lack of self-worth may cause a person to want to give up. Fear of the unknown, which includes pain and suffering, is the driving force to accelerated death. A person can decide to go this route based on their anticipation of future suffering. I have had unforgettable experiences of seeing people close to me being given a terminal diagnosis saying they trust God and lived through their suffering until the end. There is an admiration in witnessing a person live by faith, with hope, even in suffering, until God says it's time to leave here. A life lived until the very end despite it being easy is brave, and that is the *true* meaning of dying with dignity. I would like to add that they not only died with dignity, but they also died leaving a legacy of faith.

This present day we thrive off others who chose the path of faith and their stories empower us today. We remember Dr. Martin Luther King, Jr., whose life and family was threatened daily; yet he stayed the course. We remember Harriet Tubman who had the audacity to set herself free and threaten her own life by going back to free others. She had the mindset that she was either going to be free or die.

Countless others also chose to live on purpose, having faith in God during life threatening situations. They chose to live, not simply exist, or be paralyzed by life's misfortunes. They saw hope, leaned towards its light, and was strengthened by every step forward they took. Are you ready to leave a legacy of faith that will teach your children and children's children how to stand in these sometimes unbelievable days we are seeing? Choosing to live by faith will demonstrate to those left behind how to press through hard times. It enlightens others to keep holding on, never give up, and fight the good fight of faith until the very end. Suffering and death is clearly a part of life, and without faith, one can fall into despair, bitterness, anger, and hopelessness.

Living by Faith

A high-powered woman is not about being the most beautiful, the most popular, the best in everything she does, or the most accomplished according to society's standards, but one whose foundation is on the solid rock of Jesus Christ. A high-powered woman lives by faith that is fully assured in the hope of every promise of God. She believes His Word is true and will come to pass. Hebrews 11:6 says, "But without faith *it is* impossible to please *him*: for he that cometh to God must believe that he is, and *that* he is a rewarder of them that diligently seek him."

Without faith, means to be separated from God because we cannot be in relationship with him without faith. To be without means there is a void or lack in a particular area. When we are without God, there is surely a void and lack in our soul. God created us in His image and likeness and created us to be in relationship with Him. Without God, we are deprived of that relationship and experience a separation from our creator. Oftentimes we are aware of a void in our lives even when everything else is going well when we are not in a relationship with God. Think about it, when there is a separation from someone, there is a feeling of abandonment. In addition, one feels bereaved. They are in mourning. When my best friend moved away, as she drove off in her moving truck, a piece of me felt like it died. I also felt like she had abandoned me. I cried for days. The feeling was ten times worse when my father died. When a loved one dies, we often feel abandoned and bereaved. Some believe that they cannot live without their loved one.

When we are without faith, we are separated from God and grieve the loss of the relationship. We often can't quite track the feeling, but feel like something is missing in our lives. We may try to search and even cry out exclaiming our need for something that is already within us…faith! Jesus made it emphatically clear in John 14:6 when He said, "I am the way, the truth, and the life; no man cometh to the Father, but by me." He also proclaimed prior to that in John 7:37, "If any man thirsts, come to me and out of His belly will flow rivers of living water."

You see, there are many things one can believe in, but I am speaking from a personal experience of a high-powered woman who believes in Jesus Christ. There is a different kind of flow to her response to life. As I drank from the cup of truth, in time, I began to experience a transformation that I never could have imagined happening. You see, when Jesus said "out of the belly will flow rivers of living water, '' he was referring to the Holy Spirit who was to come after he ascended to be with the father. The Holy Spirit would dwell within the believer until Jesus Christ returns. Confirmation of our power is in Ephesians 3:20, "Now unto Him who is able to do exceedingly, abundantly above all we could ask or think according to the power that works in you."

A high-powered woman is unable to do life on her own, she needs a higher power to live this life, live in this world, interact with people, and to be all that God created her to be. It will indeed take the same power that raised Christ from the dead to raise you up in the weakest, darkest, and most challenging times in your life. Even in the mountain experiences, the Holy Spirit is needed to keep you in all your ways. I am amazed at so many high-powered women I have personally encountered in my lifetime who exhibited a life of faith during tumultuous times in their lives.

I know it had to be God working in them, for them, and through them. Our history books are filled with stories of high-powered women; the Bible shares stories of how they existed in situations where faith in God was their only hope.

In the fifth chapter of Mark, there is a woman who was known for having and issue with bleeding. Her actual name is not mentioned; however, she is one popular sister. Her story is so compelling and powerful. She demonstrates a living faith that perseveres through shame, pain, brokenness, isolation, rejection, confusion, financial lack, and more. Although this woman is unnamed, I would like to call her a high-powered woman.

The Bible mentions that she had an issue of blood. We know that this type of issue most likely led to a plethora of other issues. After twelve years, she was depleted of all her resources and still left with no solutions to her problem. I am sure she was extremely exhausted mentally, physically, and emotionally. But, when she heard about Jesus, she began to plan. What do you do when you have given everything you have towards the brokenness in your life? Do you have a plan to get through this? What does your bounceback look like?

Our high-powered woman in this story planned to have an encounter with Jesus. She set her heart on the goal and was determined to reach it. Jesus would soon become her Savior, Great Physician, and her Heavenly Father. Jesus would be the greatest physician she ever knew and give her the best news she had heard in a long time. She held fast to her faith, which allowed her to see her healing even before it manifested. Her plan was put in motion to discreetly move through the crowd and press her way to Jesus.

The scriptures say that she said within herself, "If I can only touch the hem of His garment, I will be made whole." You see, this living faith is one that acts even when you are tired. Even when you are not okay, when you are frustrated or unable to see the evidence of your deliverance right at that moment. Our faith speaks life and says, "I believe what was said about God in the scriptures and that through faith in Jesus Christ, I am saved." And then we speak more life: "I am in complete agreement with the Word of God. If I believe I am saved, then I must believe that all things are possible with God and that there is nothing too hard for Him." I am not sure where you are right now in your own personal issue, but I encourage you to say right where you are, "I BELIEVE God!"

You see, before our high-powered sister even got to Jesus's garment, she had already envisioned what her healing would look like. She spoke it within herself and moved forward. Oftentimes, we lack vision because we lack faith. I can't tell you how many times I missed opportunities to be blessed or be a blessing because I lacked faith in God. I chose fear over faith. The realities of life can be so overwhelming that we often turn to other people or vices to find solutions. Our behavior can easily become unrestrained as our our anger and anxiety rise, leading us away from our goal. Perhaps, we quit altogether and stop short of receiving what God has planned for us.

I wondered if after living with her condition for twelve years the woman ever thought about giving up and just dying right there in her issues like I did that night in my bedroom. But as I read her story over again, I clearly saw that her faith influenced a strong determination to live. According to Hebrews 11:1, "Faith is the substance of things hoped for, the evidence of things not seen." What did she hope for and see for her future that made her fight so hard to live? What passions were inside her that she wanted to live out? Did she believe that life had to be more than this suffering? Did she refuse to believe that this was all that life had to offer? Where did she derive her sense of self-worth in a society that saw women as lower in rank than men? To fight to live means you believe you have purpose in your living. So, I wonder what was her "why" for choosing to live and not die in her own blood.

In Leviticus 17:14, God says, "For the life of every creature is in the blood...." Therefore, this woman's life was deteriorating a little every day for twelve years as the blood drained from her body. As she finally worked her way through the crowd to Jesus, her moment was now! Yes! She got it! She touched the hem of His garment. Our high-powered woman arrived at her goal and this wasn't simply a success story, this was her life restored.

The moment she touched Jesus's garment, her flow dried up. This woman, who was declared a ceremonially unclean sinner because of her issue of blood, was cleansed. There was an exchange: her sin for His forgiveness; her blood issue for His power to heal; her faith for His all-sufficiency that redeems, cleanses, saves, and restores. This woman whose name was unknown was now known as a daughter of God.

We are no different than our high-powered sister who chose to live. God desires that we, too, will be healed. My sister, God knows your condition, your frailties, and your broken heart. He also knows that many are still in spiritual bondage and experiencing loss after loss. Throughout the scriptures, we see God's love, compassion, and mercies. God is saying, "I saw you then and I see you now." He is looking upon you with compassion. God has heard your cry. The cries from deep in your soul. Your cries to the Savior, the only God who can save you, the only God who can deliver you. He has seen your afflictions and your sorrow, has seen you wallowing in your blood, soaked in pain, and oppressed. When you cry out to Him as a child lost and afraid, covered with the burdens of life, you continued to live. Just as God declared to Israel in Ezekiel 16:6 to "live." He has given you everything that you will need to live with power by faith.

Choose to Live by Faith

How does the high-powered woman of today overcome the issues that seem to have no cure, never ending and impure? She puts her trust in God. So many people seem to have remedies for so many things. Some of their suggestions are valuable and helpful. However, we must always value above all else God's power and ability to do the impossible. Sometimes, it feels like we lack faith; however, the scriptures say that we all have a measure of faith and that all you need is faith the size of a mustard seed. Our faith has great power to help us to live.

We have a choice! The definition of *choice* from the Merriam-Webster Dictionary is "the power of choosing; care in selecting; a person or thing chosen." When we choose Jesus, we do not do so haphazardly; we do so with care and concern. The ball is in your court. You have the power of choice! Jesus has made a way for you to know Him. If you are not sure you know Him, you can learn of Him and make your own decision. Romans 10:17 says, "Faith comes by hearing and hearing by the Word of God." Our hearing is a pathway to our hearts. As we hear, our hearts can either receive or reject the information. Romans 10:9-10 says, "If you declare with your mouth, 'Jesus is Lord,' and believe in your heart that God raised him from the dead, you will be saved."

Every person lives what they believe. What do you believe? A high-powered woman lives and believes what God has said; that is how she is able to walk in power that goes beyond human understanding. She is trained by the Word of God. She stands on His promises that preserve her life. God is her hope and strength. She cannot *not* assist in ending her life because she has the light of Christ dwelling within her. "Then Jesus said, "Did I not tell you that if you believe, you will see the glory of God?" (John 11:40).

I don't know your story or what you believe, but in times like these, it is imperative to be anchored on a firm, secure, and rock-solid foundation. "For we live by faith, not by sight" (2 Corinthians 5:7). May you choose the path of faithfulness as the calming peace of God bathes you and may His favor be a sweet aroma upon every mountain you climb, every path you travel, and every wilderness experience you will face. When you choose to believe the truth and live in Christ, you have made the best decision of your life!

Chapter 3
A High-Powered Redemption

Going from ruined to redeemed is an experience and a freedom worth talking about. Ephesians 1:7 says, "In him we have redemption through his blood, forgiveness of sins, in accordance with the riches of God's grace." To be free in our soul is the most amazing feeling; to wake up every day feeling that life has no meaning or purpose is bondage. To feel no connection with the almighty creator feels like a void of uncertainty. God has the power to release us from anything that has us bound if we choose life.

Redemption was a breath of fresh air compared to the suffocating and limiting air in the pit I was in.

I was born Michelle Lamonica Todd on a warm summer day to Levert C. Todd, Sr. and Sandra L. Todd. I have two older sisters and two younger brothers. I was born and raised in the small city of Chester, Pennsylvania. For some time, we lived in government housing. Back then it was called the Projects; today it is known as public housing. Inside of our home was a large fish tank full of all types of fish that my daddy loved. Later, our dog Snapper, a German Shepherd, joined the family.

Growing up in the Todd household was truly an experience. It was a happy home and loving environment. Mom could often be found in the kitchen or hanging with Daddy in the living room, enjoying coffee and conversation. My father was super funny and loud. We were a family who loved to laugh, sing, have fun, play games, tease one another, and watch movies together. When it was movie time, we enjoyed my father's homemade stovetop popcorn. I can still hear the large pot rubbing back and forth on the electric burner as the sound of the kernels went *pop-pop*. Daddy would then put the popcorn in a large brown paper bag and add plenty of salt. We would sit on the floor in our pajamas and everyone would dig in as we watched a good movie with the lights off.

We were a family who attended church every Sunday and stayed there all day. I was often called Church Girl. On Saturdays we did chores, played outside, and went to yard sales and the well-known flea market, Cowtown. By early evening, the Sunday morning preparation began. I dreaded the time it took my mother to do my hair. But when she was done, I always loved how pretty it turned out. My father was a preacher and became an elder in the church. He was also a Bible teacher, counselor, and evangelist. My mother was supportive of us all and took great care of our home. She went back to work after my youngest brother started school. Mom was a daycare teacher for over thirty years. I always loved visiting her classroom. She was so creative, and the children loved her.

Being the middle child, I always wanted to be around my older sisters, Patrice and Levette—who was also known as Keisha. To this day, I always brag about my sissies! They are two of the prettiest, smartest, most loving and amazing women ever, besides our awesome mother. As a little girl, I would watch their every move and admire their beauty and skills. I wanted to be just like them. Unfortunately, my comparison to them was a contributing factor as to how I perceived myself. My sisters' complexions are light brown. The difference between my dark skin compared to their caramel skin was evident to me. I loved their light brown eyes and confidence. They were outgoing and popular, while I was quiet and shy. As I got older, I enjoyed seeing my elder sister, Patrice, as a talented hairdresser in school. While my middle sister, Keisha, was successful in academics, sports, theater, and other extracurricular activities. She was even the first person in our immediate family to attend college. Both of my sisters were great communicators and I wanted to be just like them. I was reminded of how impossible that was as I was teased about my dark skin, my buck teeth, and called Four Eyes because of my glasses. It's amazing how early on we see differences among people and start to compare ourselves with others.

I had a lisp from sucking my thumb. In elementary school, I had to attend speech classes to correct my speech impediment. This was embarrassing because my speech teacher would call my name as I followed her down the hall to Speech Therapy. In my view I just could not get it together. I put a lot of pressure on myself at a young age because I felt horrible about my inabilities. During a parent-teacher conference, I overheard my third grade teacher tell my mother I could read and spell very well but I could not remember or fully understand what I read. Shortly after that, I attended ECIA classes for reading comprehension and math. There they went again, calling my name for me to go down the hall to correct yet another problem. This program included individualized instruction and improved my reading comprehension skills. I began to love it. The work was easier and I could understand it. It wasn't until adulthood that I learned I was a visual and hands-on learner. It wasn't that I couldn't learn; I just learned differently than the other kids. I was always afraid in a learning environment, fearful that the teacher would call me up to the blackboard and I would not know the answer to the question they would ask. I would constantly call myself stupid, so much so that I really believed it. It is frustrating as a child to know you want to do something and can't.

I struggled with being teased about my dark skin, my struggles to tie my sneakers, and my "four eyes." I often laughed it off, but I was dying inside. The negativity worked all through my poor little soul. I even felt relief when other children were teased because at least it wasn't me this time. I would even laugh when they got bullied, even though I felt bad for them because I knew what it felt like. I remember coming home from middle school feeling sad because some boys called me Blacky. This was about twelve years old: the age when girls start to really notice boys. My father noticed my countenance and asked me what was wrong. I normally did not express my feelings, but that day I told him what the boys called me. My father looked me in the eyes and said, "What?" He looked around as if he didn't want anyone to know what he was going to say next. Then he whispered , "Don't tell anyone, but you are my favorite." I can't express the joy I felt as he continued: "Do you know why?

"No," I replied.

"Because you are black just like your mother. Do you know why I married your mother?" he asked.

"No."

"Because she is a beautiful black queen. Baby girl, you don't see it now, but when you get older, men are going to love your beautiful black skin."

My daddy spoke these words with such boldness, strength, and confidence. Although I still could not see my beauty, I walked away from that conversation believing that even if no one else thought I was beautiful, my father sure did. I believed his words because he always showed great affection towards my mother. And I, too, thought my mother was a beautiful woman.

After his passing, my siblings and I laughed, remembering how he told us all we were his favorite and why. He loved us all the same for different reasons. Daddy was a confident man and always told us to be strong as black people. He was steadfast in building up others. He never wanted us or others to feel inferior as a black person and how God created us. If he were here today, I'm sure he would be so proud of his family. It is amazing how persuasive our perception is and how it can influence our emotions and behavior.

In tenth grade, I met a guy who showed a sincere interest in me and we started dating. He was a gentleman, loved my dark skin, and accepted me just as I was. This happened around the time my family faced a great tragedy that turned our world upside down. I was deeply impacted, but of course, life keeps going on, and mental health check-ins were not employed in those days. However, it was good to have a temporary escape from life's prevailing issues with my new boyfriend.

My confidence was boosted, and I found a special reason to smile. My dark skin was often overlooked and rejected, so I was shocked to have someone who was genuinely attracted to my beauty. We dated, fell in love, and at sixteen years old at the end of my junior year, I learned that I was pregnant. I gave birth to my son at the age of seventeen, during my senior year. Not too long after we graduated, my son's father and I broke up and that devastated me. I was broken, vulnerable, and insecure. About nine months later, I met someone who was about five years older than I who had a car and an apartment. He seemed to be mature, nice, and a hard worker. I felt beautiful and believed I was in love…again.

It was the end of spring when I moved out of my parents' home and right into a dysfunctional and chaotic environment. My main reason for leaving was that I did not want to abide by my parents' rules of having a curfew, doing chores, and being respectful of their home. Oh, what toils and snares we find ourselves in when we are not obedient to our parents. Living in my parents' home was a covering and a protection from a lot of things I did not know were lingering in the streets. I complained of their strict rules and wanted to do my own thing. I learned quickly that the term *these streets* ain't *loyal* is the truth.

I was pulled into this man's world and got involved in illegal drug activities that I was not built for. I experienced physical, emotional, and sexual abuse with this guy that impacted me long after the relationship ended. The act of abuse is violent to endure as it can take you to a different kind of low. For me, it did more than startle me on the inside; it stirred up a greater fear that exacerbated an already shaken soul and produced a feeling of death. Even a simple look of rage is traumatizing because you know something bad is coming next, but you don't know *what* until it happens. This time in my life triggered a jumpiness and anxiousness within me that stayed with me for a very long time.

During this time, my appearance started to decline and I was giving up on my education. I was attending business school at the time and I could not even function in class; I missed assignments, and almost failed my classes. I will never forget how my best friend, Sheri, the one who helped teach me how to tie my sneakers stepped in, pulled me out of the rut I was in, spoke to my professors, and helped me make it to graduation. It was an extremely dark time in my life as I was separated from everything that was right, safe, peaceful, and hopeful.

Once, Patrice and her best friend popped up at the apartment and yelled my name up at the second-floor window from her car. It was summertime so the windows were open, and I heard her voice immediately. I flew downstairs at the speed of lightning because I did not want her to come inside and witness my living conditions. As I walked towards my sister, she looked me up and down and said abruptly with an attitude, "You look dusty."

She was always able to tell when something was not right with me and I would always lie. The sad part was I did look dusty. I had my graveclothes on for real. I still remember the outfit I wore in the heat of that summer: a black, faded shirt and black, faded jeans. My hair was an entire mess and my countenance looked troubled. I was so embarrassed I can't even remember my response to my sister or the conversation after that. I tried to keep my life a secret from my family, until things got really bad.

One day it occurred to me: "My own father never treated me this way. He never abused me, laid a hand on me, or called me anything other than Baby Girl or Shellfish." In addition, I never witnessed my father abuse my mother or disrespect her or my sisters. I put the little bit of pride I had left aside and called my mother, asking her if I could come home. Her words to me were "Yes, your room is still the same." She also reminded me that I had to abide by the house rules. I moved back home but continued to see my boyfriend until things got so bad, there was no way I could continue being in the relationship. My life was at stake. Breaking away from the relationship was difficult emotionally. It was not only low self-worth and low self-esteem, this was indeed spiritual warfare and the mind battles that kept me in the pit. But it was God's grace that saved me.

Lo and behold, there is something about the need for acceptance and the lack of worth that will always keep you thirsting for attention. Even after returning home, I still lived a life of drama. I moved out again and a few years later, I had a second child, my daughter. Her father and I got married. Carrying a boatload of baggage, not understanding who I was, and having no clue what the marriage covenant was all about, and we could not make it work. Unfortunately, I was divorced by twenty-nine, a single mother with two children and two baby daddies.

Entering an adulterous relationship with a married man was another kind of low and it ended up lasting longer than I could have imagined. The things we tell ourselves to justify sin only lead the way to destruction. This relationship looked glamorous, yet it was destroying me on the inside because my character was a disgrace. Although I had advanced career-wise, I was simply existing and not living. I was depressed and hid it well. My outer appearance and my smile reflected a well-put-together woman who was happy and had her life in order. I continued my journey through life and got entangled in a hot mess. I realized that I always felt powerless throughout life, and that mindset led me to always believing I was a complete failure and a coward.

After five years, I was convicted of my lifestyle after attending a small group for women at church. Soon after, I ended the adulterous relationship. During that separation, I reflected on my entire life. I had so much hate towards myself, regret, guilt, shame, and low self-worth. My very soul was tormented. Satan used my sins against me. He loaded me down with guilt and shame and tempted me with thoughts of ending it all. You see, he knew more about me than I did. He knew I was loved by God, because it is written that "God so loved the *world*, that he gave his only begotten son, that whosoever believes in him will not perish, but have everlasting life." Satan remembered when I got saved at the age of ten during Sunday school. That day when my best friend's mother, Evangelist Dorothy Bruton, taught us about Jesus Christ and then asked who wanted to be saved. I raised my hand, and she stopped the class and took me to the altar. I repeated the words of salvation and she prayed with me. I was saved that day. And yes, the day I was baptized too; he saw it all.

You see, Satan knew all about the words I had written in my journals over the years begging God to help me. I bet he heard the spirit-filled prayers of my grandmother, mother, and whoever else was praying for me. I was valued and Satan knew it. This was an attack on my life and at my very lowest, God's grace stepped in and my Savior said, "ENOUGH!"

It was just like the divine encounter Jesus had with the woman at the well. That moment changed the entire trajectory of her life. But, it was more than the encounter, it was the gift Jesus offered her. He told her in John 4:10: "If you only knew the gift God has for you and who you are speaking to, you would ask me, and I would give you living water." Later, Jesus clarifies that He is that gift. He is the one to quench our very thirst, bring us into all truth, and build up our confidence. Through Jesus, we are filled with a divine purpose along with the desire and power to carry it out. It is He who is our very life in whom we live, move, and have our being. It is Jesus Christ who will be the one to save us from our sins and bring us into eternal life with God.

Jesus was the one to open the eyes of this broken, rejected, and abandoned woman at the well. I believe she felt what I felt in me that night I had an encounter with the Lord: the feeling of restoration, redemption, hope, strength, forgiveness, unspeakable joy, peace, and a connection that was missing the entire time. That night was my high-powered comeback. The redemptive power of God was upon me and no devil, obstacle, or person was going to stop the plans He had for me.

Therefore, my high-powered sister, it is your time to rise from the ashes, get out of those dirty garments, be real about your new nature, and live unapologetically. To my sister who has been there and done that, let's praise God together and continue to remember our high-power comeback and help the next sister along the way. This is monumental and supernatural. It is possible to come back from anything—yes, anything you have experienced. There is nothing we can't overcome with the power of God in us.

Over time, so much has happened to us and in our lives. Our experiences, false belief system, and pessimistic mindset, have driven us. It takes work to unveil who we truly are, but when we discover who we are...watch out, because *the high-powered woman* has gotten her bounce back. She is not who you knew her to be; she is better than ever, and the best is yet to come.

It is by the grace and mercies of God we are here and able to be the high-powered women we are with a high-powered comeback! So, stand strong on God's forgiveness, His Word, and the masterpiece He created you to be. You may not have started out the way you would have liked, but the finish can still be amazing because God's comeback game is strong! "Therefore, there is no condemnation for those who are in Christ Jesus" (Romans 8:1).

Chapter 4
A High-Powered Confidence

I cannot tell you how many times that after a person got to know me, they confessed that they did not like me when they met me. It was either my confident walk, tall stature in high heels, my broad smile, style of dress, or the upbeat tone of my voice. I was often called "bougie," "a diva," or simply "fake." This impacted me deeply because the truth is, I never thought any of those things about myself. I did not look down on others and surely did not think I was better than anyone. This was naturally who I was. I would try to convince others that my entire family is the same way.

I remember starting a new job, and by the third week, a coworker asked me why I dressed up every day. I replied, "This is what I love to wear. I don't dress for other people; I dress for me." She had a shocked look, mixed with a dash of offense all over her face. Once I was preparing for an interview and I was told to be sure not to sashay in with all my happiness and to tone down my look. Really? Because of this, I found that over the years I began to tone down my joy if I was around joyless people. In addition, if I received a compliment about my appearance, I was quick to explain that my outfit was less expensive than they expected, simply so I could be accepted. In conversations, if I knew something, I wouldn't share it, so as to not seem like a know-it-all. Accentuating my flaws so others could feel comfortable and not intimidated by me was something I often did. I still catch myself doing it today. It was uncomfortable accepting compliments; I would redirect the conversation. I am still learning to simply say, "Thank you." I must admit, that is tough for me. My sisters, it is okay to accept the blessings we receive. Even an encouraging word is major on a bad day or during a rough season.

Now on the other hand, I would encounter women who admired and complimented my confident look, style, and positivity. There were women who built me up, encouraged me, and even saw things in me that I did not see. These women even saw through the smile, beyond the makeup, and would speak words of affirmation to my soul. I learned that there are two types of people: the confident and the unconvinced.

The confident woman can relate to any woman and sit at any table. She can connect in any circle. She can accept the success, beauty, and confidence of another woman. She is sure-footed and certain of her abilities. She is secure, satisfied, courageous, and trusted. The confident woman is humble and grateful.

The unconvinced woman is doubtful, insecure, and untrustworthy. She is highly suspicious of other women. She doesn't believe the confident woman is who she appears to be. The unconvinced woman seeks to tear her down. She is a gossiper. Her goal is to prove that the confident woman has flaws, is a fraud, or that her life is not that great. She is overwhelmingly critical and unable to speak one good thing about that confident woman. The unconvinced woman is indecisive and wavering in her relationships. She likes a person one minute and as soon as someone influential gossips about that person, she will quickly switch sides. You will find her in and out of circles, unstable and desperate to be confident herself. She sees the success of the confident woman and desires it. Unfortunately, her insecurity, jealousy, and constant comparison of herself to others prevents her from truly enjoying who she is and the life she has been blessed to maintain and even enhance.

Judging a book by its cover alone can lead to misjudgment. I believe that one of the greatest disconnects of humanity occurs when we fail to really connect and understand one another. When we don't, we fail to listen intently to each other and we make too many broad assumptions with little truth. We become critical, intimidated, jealous, and even malicious. This is a hard issue to eradicate because many lack self-awareness to the point that they don't realize they lack identity and/or are insecure within. We even find ourselves trying to outdo one another or to prove that our hardships in life were harder than another person's. Insecurity is pervasive amongst women and the pernicious ways of the jealous have divided us even in the body of Christ.

Because of the pressure of society, many women feel the need to look like those women who are on the covers of magazines or on television before they can feel confident about themselves. One may believe that confidence comes from the ability to do things perfectly, to be highly educated, or to be deemed successful by others. It's not easy to admit that you lack confidence because you fear that you will not be accepted. It is believed that if you have a level of confidence, money, connections, and an extravagant look, you can go far. Unfortunately, we have too much focus on what appears to be rather than what is. After years of living with a poor view of myself, I was an entire mess. I was messy and stayed in a mess. I was unassuming because I wasn't loud and boisterous, but yes, I could mess a thing up. To be self-aware of who we are to the core is powerful.

One must admit that they are insecure and not in a good place in life. In our desire to be confident, we must submit to the transformational work of the Holy Spirit and knowledge of who we are in God. It takes work on our end; however, with God, all things are possible. Connecting with other high-powered women, and listening to wise counsel, you will go through a purging process and arrive at a place of pure joy and contentment when you know who you are in Christ Jesus. It is possible and you will see the fruits of your hard work and the power of God, who will be everything you need in the process.

I can identify with both types of women because I have been on both sides of the spectrum. It wasn't until I believed what God said about me and who I was as a daughter of the King that caused a strong transformation in my thoughts, emotions, behavior, and my relationships. A high-powered confidence is necessary to live in this world and to fulfill all that God has planned for us. But, before one can walk in their high-powered confidence, they must know who they are and who they are not.

A very fundamental question that is not easy to answer is "Who are you?" This is a top question I ask my clients as a life coach. It is crucial to know the answer; otherwise, you may not be living your life, but someone else's. There can be a lack of authenticity in your character, leading you to become a people-pleaser to those you connect with.

If you have no true sense of identity, fear will be quick to jump into the driver's seat of your life. You may find yourself constantly worried about other people's opinions of you. Perhaps, the struggle to make decisions stresses you out because you are too afraid to make a mistake. The need to be excellent and perfect has burned you out. Your need to seek approval is at an all-time high as you chase relationship after relationship. Or run to fulfill the needs of others while neglecting your own just to be validated and feel valued.

Yes, "who are you?" is indeed a heavy question to answer. One might immediately begin to ponder as they search within, only to come up with the response: "I don't know." Some may pause, take a deep breath, search within themselves, and respond timidly, whispering a few *ums* or a *hmm*. Others give a response off the top of their head just to say something. Then there are a few who pause, roll their head to the left, then to the right, and look up to the sky, praying for the answer to be released from the heavens somehow; but, when their help doesn't come, they make a series of elongated mumbles under their breath only to say, "Can you repeat the question?" Why is "who are you?" such a hard question to answer? Well, I can tell you from my own personal experience that it is indeed a hard question when you simply just don't know.

Knowing who you are is knowing your identity in God, not what others have told you about yourself. God has the first and final say on this matter. My favorite scripture that reminds me who I am is in 2 Corinthians 5:17: "Therefore, if anyone is in Christ, he is a new creation, the old has passed away, behold the new has come." I am new in Christ. I have a new nature, a new mindset, and a new way of living, new relationships, new goals, new ideas, and a new hope. It's a brand-new me.

Can you relate to this scripture? Are you brand-new? How does it feel? How excited are you to be who you are in Christ with confidence?

Identity is a common topic at women's conferences and events. There are all types of biblical teachings and information out there regarding identity. This is necessary because we should know the importance of knowing our identity. It distinguishes one person from another. We are all different, and that is so amazing to me. A person who knows their identity and is secure in it will have a high-powered confidence. The significance of knowing your identity brings more resolve, joy, understanding, self-control, resistance to compromise, and the ability to make integral decisions. Without this knowledge, we can create a multiplicity of problems we discussed earlier.

Identity, as defined by the *Merriam-Webster Dictionary*, is the distinguishing character, personality of an individual, biological make-up, and several variations that differ from one person to another. The word *distinguishing* is significant as it means distinctive, extraordinary, or different. Oh, what peace a person can enjoy when they fully live a unique personified life. Otherwise, we will conform to whatever looks good, sounds good, and feels good without a basis of truth or honor.

Our identity in God produces the high-powered confidence necessary in life to align with His good, perfect, and acceptable plan for us. Identity lays the groundwork for building confidence and overcoming common barriers that invade our path to reaching our destiny. One who knows and accepts who they are is given access to a whole new world of living intentionally with limitless opportunities to live abundantly, serve God, and help others. But until then, the cycles of confusion, frustration, and fraudulent behavior continue. Who knows this to be true? Yours truly.

"For no one can lay any foundation other than
the one already laid, which is Jesus Christ"

(1 Corinthians 3:11).

The Bible speaks to a high degree about our identity. But it wasn't until my encounter with God on my bedroom floor that I began to long to understand who I was. I started the journey of connecting more with Christians. Learning who I was and most importantly who I was in Jesus Christ was liberating for me. From that point on, so much of me continues to be unveiled: some good, some bad, some amazing, some unexpected. The good news is the pressure of being like someone else is gone and the high-powered confidence is such freedom.

The Mask

As women, we hide a lot. We often carry guilt and shame from our past. Harbored feelings of regret and unworthiness obstruct the pathway to enjoying the favor and blessings from God and others. We often hide from the world because it can feel like everyone knows our little secret. Some gently pull back from others, afraid of getting too close. They intentionally live their lives in the background.

People often say, "I am a background person." For some, this is true. This is who they are and who they have always been. Everyone does not desire to be in the public eye and some people are less sociable than others. But others proclaim they are background people because they are hiding. They fear being exposed for whatever it is they believe they are lacking or whatever it is they are concealing.

I remember sitting in the very last row at a church I attended because I was hiding. I was hiding my sin, the real me, the person I thought would not be approved of by others. If I sat in the front, those behind me would see that I was a fraud and I would be exposed as not being a real Christian. So I dressed up every Sunday, arrived at church, sat in the back pew, and was out the door immediately after the benediction. I couldn't even worship because I didn't have a connection with God, gratitude, or even an understanding of His grace.

My sister Keisha asked me one Sunday why I wasn't worshipping during service, I just brushed off her question with a shrug. In addition, she would often try to get us to sit closer to the front and we declined. At one point, she told us that she wanted to be closer to it and kindly started sitting in another section. I don't blame her one bit. We must be confident and go after what is in our hearts. It's amazing how people can hold you back from getting your blessing, moving forward, and receiving out of life what is for you. We were holding her back from getting her blessing Sunday after Sunday. My sister took a bold initiative to move forward.

A mask is worn as a disguise to conceal identity, amuse, or terrify others. There are emotional masks we wear as well that hide our true character and emotions. My personality was what people saw first. But my character took more time to uncover. That was my true identity that I hid very well behind my friendliness and deceptive charm. I didn't want who I was behind closed doors to ever be exposed beyond my close circle.

Over the years, I have encountered women who were just like me. I have also encountered women who were mean, aggressive, controlling, angry, and bullies. However, deep down, they were afraid of being hurt, controlled, identified as weak, and bullied themselves. They created this monstrous mask to terrify others and keep them at a distance. This monstrous persona protected the wearer and repelled any who would stand in their way. This type of mask reminds me of the beast from Beauty and the Beast. Beyond this mask was a gentle giant with a fear of rejection.

Another type of mask amuses others and distracts them with an exaggerated playful manner. This includes people who put down themselves in a joking way or appeal to others' sense of humor to divert their attention from the truth. Some masks are worn to hide, some to push away, and some to present an identity that is acceptable to society or in certain circles.

Wearing a mask is not always a bad thing if we are self-aware enough to recognize ourselves and areas in which we need to get help and healing. Growth and development is an ongoing process in each of us. The reason I say this is because unmasking before just anyone is not wise. Everyone cannot handle what is underneath your mask, nor are they equipped to help you after you remove it. They may not have the compassion or understanding to meet you where you are and help bring you to a place of safety. We are so quick to tell people to take off the mask, but ladies, I recommend that you do not unveil so easily. Do not become vulnerable in front of just anyone, yet seek the Lord and wise counsel first. Proverbs 11:14 says, "Where there is no guidance, a people fall, but in an abundance of counselors there is safety."

Lastly, when another sister is in the presence of others and forces herself to smile and hold her head up, that does not mean she is fake. *This is a high-powered move* when a woman chooses to exercise emotional discipline. She is making the decision to NOT disrupt someone's peaceful atmosphere and over-obligate them to pay attention to a problem they can't understand, or remedy. No, she is not okay at the moment and does not need to tell the entire world. Sister girl already knows that when she gets home, she is going to unleash whatever is behind her mask. Perhaps, it is to give herself a good ol' cry and get the help she needs to take care of herself. A mask can serve as a covering for the time needed to get yourself together.

Each person is different. Some may need to share their problems to get catharsis, while others choose to handle their situation privately. The important thing is that both kinds of women are getting the help they need. *The mask is like a hat on a bad-hair day* that simply conceals the potential for beauty that lies underneath. All it needs is a professional's touch. I cannot stress enough the importance of knowing your identity in God because then you will know the difference between masking your identity and true character versus choosing not to disclose a season of suffering. Everything is not for everybody.

People often tell me that I seem to be so free. The good news is that I am free in Christ and free to be everything God created me to be. My confidence is not in my appearance but in who I am in the Lord, my purpose, and the overwhelming fact that Christ is my Savior.

We all have moments of insecurity and that is to be expected. But in those moments, we must remember to apply the truth to every thought and reject every lie. Your self-esteem comes from being confident in who you are and who God says you are. You are more than enough because the Bible says you are fearfully and wonderfully made. Hold your head up, my sister, broaden your smile, and secure your stride. Go forth with a high-powered confidence and prosper as God wills!

Chapter 5
A High-Powered Purpose

Lift up your eyes. Your heavenly Father waits to bless you--
in inconceivable ways to make your life
what you never dreamed it could be.

--Anne Ortlund

God has a divine purpose and a plan for each and every one of us. A purpose-filled life is never regretted when it is the Will of God. There are many things we can recall regretting in our lifetime; but fulfilling our purpose is not one of them. One of the most life-changing and monumental years in my life was 2012. This is the year that the revelations spoken directly to me from God were so prominent and powerful. The timeline of events in my life was intended by God. It was a continuation of the transformational process that would now catapult me into my purpose. Through the pit extraction, character development, and my own personal wilderness experience, I was blossoming. I was intrigued by the cute new buds forming from this new nature I was in.

God was molding and shaping me into a vessel that would be suitable for Him and prepared to do good works. But before God could release crucial instructions to me, I had to be ready to hear and obey every word. God was very precise during this season of my life. Obedience, faith, and courage would be necessary to move forward. Obedience is a direct connection with God and keeps us on the path He has prepared for us.

A purpose-filled life is not about becoming rich, taking trips, having my name called by great men and women—nor is it about having a seat in high places. It is to hear directly from God and walk with Him. These things may come in process, but that process should never be our focus. My focus is to accept the assignment God gave me and to make it my mission to fulfill it.

To have a clearer picture of our God-created purpose, we can study Jesus's ministry here on earth. He made it clear who He was and why He came: "to seek and save the lost." He also said in Luke 4:18, "The spirit of the Lord is upon me, because He has anointed me to preach the gospel to the poor; He has sent me to heal the brokenhearted, to proclaim liberty to the captives and recovery of sight to the blind, to set at liberty those who are oppressed." Through Jesus's ministry, we learn how to be confident, firm, and committed to fulfilling the plan of God. We also observe how He was received and rejected, loved and hated, accused and abused, lied about and sold out.

Living a purpose-filled life is rewarding because we know we have fulfilled our Kingdom purpose. This will be accomplished by the divine power of God. There will be a fullness within us and within each day with the desire to execute what God has spoken and placed in our hearts. Our spirits are more settled, which brusquely stops the search for needing to know why we were even born. Yet we must be clear we are doing what God has called us to do. Why is this important? Because you will be challenged by Satan, people, and your own self at times. You will be able to stand firm and flatfooted knowing you are in the Will of God. It wasn't until 2012 that I was ready to get ready for what was to come.

In April of 2012, I joined a new church and guess what, my sisters? I was sitting closer to the front of it. At the end of April, on the thirtieth day to be exact, came a day I will never forget. I got up that morning and went for a walk. I enjoyed my experience in nature and just began to thank God for all His morning wonders. I just admired things such as the birds chirping and playing with one another; the beautiful lawns that housed lovely plants and flowers; even the fluffy clouds that captured my thoughts of the heavens. I wondered what God was doing beyond the clouds.

I began to talk out loud to Him: "God, what are you doing right now? Are you creating something beautiful for today? Did you see me walking through the neighborhood and could you feel my excitement for this day you made?"

In that moment, the Lord spoke to my heart these words: "*As you were admiring me, I was admiring you, your smile, your stride, my beautiful masterpiece.*" These words caused me to stop in my tracks and run home. I remember sharing them with my mother, who advised me to write this moment down.

That evening, I dropped my daughter off at dance class and hurried home to prepare for work the next day. I immediately felt an urge to pray, but I wanted to finish what I was doing first. How many of you have been there? Well, a few minutes later, I felt the urge again, and after the third time, I heard "*PRAY NOW!*" I realized this was God moving in my spirit and speaking to my heart. I remember hitting the Power Off button on the television so fast as I immediately got on my knees to pray. I thought I was going to do all the talking, but God had something important to say to me. I then heard these words within: "*You are going to be my messenger. Go back to school. You are an evangelist. You are going to be a writer and I love you so much.*" He began to fill my heart with so much love—it was overwhelming. While my eyes were closed,

I saw things of beauty; a calmness and peace came over me. I began to cry uncontrollable tears of joy and gratitude. I remember saying aloud, "Thank you, Lord! I have never felt a love like this before." What was even more amazing was that this took place in the very room where God met me during the lowest point of my life just a few years prior, calling my name and telling me He would never leave me or forsake me.

The next month, I was rushing to work one morning. I was running late and *boom*, I got stuck at a light. I started to panic because this was a long light I always dreaded. While waiting for it to change, I heard the words *"I am redeeming the time in your life!"* I don't remember what I felt at that moment, but what I know now is that those prophetic words surely came to pass. God was moving quickly in my life in a variety of ways and areas that I didn't quite understand and those around me sure didn't either. But obedience remained my guide.

By the end of May 2012, I was the worship leader at a Friday night revival. I was still battling fear hard but I prayed through the fear the entire time. My mother and my boyfriend Brandon were a strong force in my life during that time of transformation. Brandon and I continued to *date and wait*, learning each other and growing more in love. My love for God was expanding each day. I was still in Bible school and learning more than ever. I was attending various women's conferences and God was showing me something about Him, myself, my relationships, and more at each one.

Let me pause and say this: I will always encourage women's events and conferences led by God. There are so many in need of spiritual healing and I needed each one of those events, as God used various anointed women to empower and inspire me in many ways. I was beginning to connect with different women. The circles of people in my life were changing; it was all happening so fast. I went back to college and joined the evangelism ministry at church, as God instructed. In my journal, I was writing feverishly, recording much of my journey. Everything God told me to do, I did it--totally afraid. Earlier that year I read Joyce Meyer's book *Do It Afraid*. I had battled with fear for so long and this book helped me understand fear, how to fight fear, and how to move forward by faith. (I have this small book in my nightstand to this day.) Day after day, I kept moving in faith. There was a boldness and confidence building inside of me that I didn't quite understand, but God was behind it all. He was shaping a high-powered woman with a high-powered purpose.

Purpose is what each of us are called to. Purpose is the reason something exists. Each person was created on purpose by God for a purpose. There is power in knowing who you are, why you were created, and what you were created to do. Not understanding purpose creates confusion in a person's life. It can cause them to always feel something is missing, that they lack direction and value and are simply existing in life instead of living intentionally. One of my favorite scriptures that highlights what we are created to do is in Ephesians 2:10: "For we are God's handiwork, created in Christ Jesus to do good works, which God prepared in advance for us to do." God already prearranged our purpose and destiny. We were not saved merely for our own profit or benefit, but to build up and edify the church.

As believers in Jesus Christ and high-powered women, filled with the Holy Spirit, we are part of the family of God and are all called to do good works. It is written in the Bible that we are to feed the hungry, pray for others, visit the prisoners and the sick, and take care of the widow and the orphans. God has chosen us to be His ambassadors to go forth and spread the good news of Jesus Christ through whom all people can be saved. First Peter 2:9 says, "But you are a chosen race, a royal priesthood, a holy nation, a people for his own possession, that you may proclaim the excellencies of him who called you out of darkness into his marvelous light."

One of my assignments is to help others discover their God-given purpose. This is inspired through a person knowing who they are in Christ, as well as their spiritual gifts, skills, and talents. These all impact how we fulfill God's plan for each of our lives.

At a workshop on spiritual gifts I attended, the facilitator was adamant about each person knowing what their specific gifts were and walking in their spiritual giftedness. I went home and called my mother, asking her if she knew what my gift was. She said I could bake a delicious pound cake and pointed out how I love to write. I was like, "Nah, those are my hobbies." I then called my sister Patrice, who mentioned that I like to run, and I was like, "Nah, that's a sport."

Patrice paused and then said that when we talk, she always felt a sense of healing. She mentioned that I could have the gift of healing and that it didn't necessarily have to be healing of the hands. Something clicked and I remembered an elder of the church prophesying to me one Sunday morning at church that I had the gift of healing. After my conversation with Patrice, I thought about the many people over the years who expressed how much I encouraged them when we talked. I went deeper and thought about the clients I served over the years who found themselves comfortable talking to me and releasing all types of pains, hurts, tears, and sharing their dreams. I went even further back and recalled that in middle school, my girlfriend named me Dear Gossip. I was supposed to be a replica of "Dear Abby," a woman who had an advice column in the daily newspaper. As Dear Gossip, my friends would slip me notes before, during, or after school asking for advice. I remember one note so clearly that said, "Dear Gossip, I like this boy in seventh grade, but I am afraid to say something to him. What should I do?" I responded with a note giving my advice. I know, hilarious, right?

I still laugh about it to this day. After those conversations with my sister and mother, my memory jogged, I realized there was something brewing within me that had always been there.

As time went on, my eyes were open, and I was on a search to be able to define my purpose clearly. One day, I was assisting a client in defining her goals and the barriers she had that were preventing her from achieving her goals. After our interview, she left feeling so excited to return to school, get a good job, save money, and purchase a home one day. Her entire countenance had changed and the hope she had leaving my presence had my little soul leaping with joy and laughter like a bunch of children jumping high on a trampoline. I discovered my purpose right there at that moment. I realized that God had created me with a desire to hear people's problems and an even greater desire to want to help them solve these problems. I wanted people to be well and whole. I always felt the desire to help people and even save them from whatever troubles they were facing. I even had mercy on the meanest and most wicked people. I noticed how it was even difficult for me to hold a grudge. I then remembered my career as a life coach and all the people I helped over the years and *boom*, it hit me: *I was called to help others.* At this point in my life, I was living my God-given purpose and carrying out the mission of helping others through my career, serving on the evangelism ministry and doing community outreach, posting encouraging posts on Facebook, praying for women, and giving Bibles to people who did not have one. I was excited as God moved like lightning upon my heart so I would be open to His plans as he expanded my territory.

God expands our territory when we simply obey Him and carry out the mission connected to our purpose that aligns with His will. The scriptures teach us that the purpose of the body of Christ is to worship God above all else, carry out His will by helping others and building up His kingdom, and to do good works. Along with a purpose, God gives each person a mission and the vision to carry out their purpose. We can do this by the power of the Holy Spirit, faith, and by using our individual gifts, talents, and skills. That is why it is important to *know* so that you can *go* forth with confidence as a high-powered woman with purpose and God's plan.

Beware of the Purpose Blockers

When you are clear about the path you should take with the specific assignment that aligns with God's purpose for humankind, you will encounter many barriers and blocks. Be aware of the three S's: Society, Satan, and Self.

Society

People will simply be people, and some will hold you to their rigid standards. You will encounter people who will judge you, then label you and be very critical of every step you take. Some are unaware of their insecurities and will project them on you as well. They may push for you to be perfect in every way while you carry out your assignment. Some have fixed mindsets and restricted belief systems that will keep you locked in to their plans for you. Listen very carefully: if you do not know who you are in God, your spiritual gifts, talents, skills, and the vision and mission God has shown you, then you will be bound to people and not God. You will live for others and not God. You will live under people's commands and not God's. We all should have a pastor, mentor, good friend, counselor, etc. to be a guide and to give us wise counsel; however, we must be able to hear from God who will establish the path we should take. God must be the final authority, and anyone added to that process will confirm what He already says.

One evening, I received a call, and the conversation was more than I bargained for. Back then, I was more established in ministry and clear on my assignment from God. The conversation went to the left as the person who called began to question everything about me. They questioned my intentions, my education, my ministry, my business, and even my presence on social media. I remember being completely shocked and stumped at how this conversation was going. The words that screamed the loudest in my ears were *"I didn't mean to crush your dreams."* At that snide remark, I was alerted in my spirit that this was an attack to frustrate my purpose.

We don't always know what is in other people's hearts and why they say and do what they do; however, the enemy used that opportunity to try to cause discord. I kindly responded to that statement in love: "This is not a dream; I am doing it and it is a call from God."

This person emphasized a lot of traditional advice that could not be backed up with scripture. This is why I push so very hard for Christians to know the Bible, God's attributes, and so much more. I had witnessed the fruit of what God was doing in my life as well as other people's lives through the ministry and other assignments I was called to carry out; therefore, I was able to respond with confidence and in love.

That evening I learned on another level about the importance of KNOWING what God has said and to be confident in it. Although I was very hurt by this phone call, I had a stronger desire to help others be clear on what they are created to do, build up their confidence, and to help them KNOW beyond a shadow of a doubt that they are significant. It is important to know that healing is much faster when you are in connection with God.

We don't stay in that moment; we keep pressing on to what is next. My brother, Lamarr, taught me this. He is a comedian and experienced with situations, events, and people. He once said, "No matter what happens, it is what it is. You learn from it and move on to the next thing." It is also clear to me that when you know God, believe God, walk in obedience, and trust Him through the good and the bad, then the naysayers who only care what society says, who are fixated on traditions and their own perspective will not stop what God has ordained for you from when you were within your mother's womb. Be strong, be humble, and stay close to the heart of God; He will strengthen you.

SATAN

We know we are to beware of Satan because he is a liar, accuser, and purpose-frustrater. The enemy will draw our attention away from God and what we should be doing for Him. He will remind us of our past, our mistakes, and tell us how much of a failure we are. His goal is to stop us from doing the will of God. He will whisper lies that sound so good and will try to mix God's word in it; therefore, they will sound believable to the one who lacks knowledge.

We are encouraged to fear not and to not be dismayed. We must know the truth that will empower us through the toughest times of life. James 4:7 says, "Submit, therefore to God. Resist the devil and he will flee from you." Our submission to God is protection from Satan's snare. We learn how to overcome the snares of the enemy by keeping on the whole armor of God knowing that nothing can stop His plan for your life. We will discuss this in greater depth in the next chapter.

SELF

High-powered women, the work we do is not drudgery or a chore; it is victory. We cannot allow what seem to be setbacks to create a negative mindset about our assignments. If we agree with negativity, this will greatly hinder our ability to see our strengths and gifts or even to believe we are chosen.

My sister, purpose is within you. Continue to seek God and commit to serving the Kingdom and greater will you see and do. Purpose is a motivator for living. It is the strong passion that is burning within to fulfill something that impacts others in a positive way and pleases the heart of God. We stop ourselves from moving forward because we allowed Satan, society, and our own barriers to block us from achieving everything we were assigned to do. We either don't start, don't finish, or are too afraid to go any further than where we are now. God gives us the ability to produce through the work of the Holy Spirit that works with us to succeed in all things godly. A high-powered woman walks in her God-given purpose and produces!

The high-powered woman is committed to the obligation of living *on purpose* in her God-given purpose. She shows up each day. Are you showing up? Are you obligated to God? Are you obligated to care for yourself so that you can have a healthy mind, body, and spirit on this journey called life?

Many people are obligated to everything from their children, to the job, to their spouse, and when it comes to God and themselves, they don't show up as they would for others. Why is this? Why do we fight so hard for others but are ready to throw in the towel when it comes to ourselves, our dreams, our desires, or our hopes? Some of us lack commitment in our own spiritual and personal development, while some have insufficient knowledge of God and are complacent about what they already know. In either case, there is no desire to grow. Our dedication has died to defeat and despair, and death of something or someone, perhaps herself. When we commit to something, we trust there will be a favorable outcome. My sister, don't give up on purpose. Believe God, be patient, stay on the path of righteousness, and watch as well as pray. Live out your high-powered purpose.

Today is not just my responsibility; but,
an opportunity to do better in life.

-- Michelle Primeaux

Chapter 6
A High-Powered Warrior

But thanks be to God! He gives us the victory
through our Lord Jesus Christ.

--1 Corinthians 15:57

Great are the vicissitudes of our human experience. Not one person is exempt from them. Even the most anointed, faithful, hardworking, wealthy, educated, beautiful and statuesque person at some point will find themselves in a grievous place; from feeling as though they are God's best friend and most favored child to feeling like His worst enemy. You may go from feeling as high as Moses on Mount Sinai, and dancing like David before God, to feeling as low as Mephibosheth in Lo-debar.

Life will have you singing sweet praises one day and the next day experiencing bitter circumstances that are so great that you can easily question your entire existence. You may feel sorry for yourself, and throw a perpetual pity party by invitation only, with a heart that is cold and bitter. We have read in scripture about the stormy circumstances of the many Bible characters on their journeys. We learned about the host of tears from the woman with the alabaster box who wept at Jesus's feet after living a life of sin. We read about Jacob wrestling with God after being on the run from his brother. At some point, we may have felt bad about the laborious journey and the many battles the children of Israel had to face. And as we look at our own personal lives, I'm sure we can confess that we, too, have cried out to God at some point, asking Him at least one of the following questions: *Where are you, God? What am I to do, God? When will it be over, God? Why did this happen to me, God? Do you see me? How am I going to make it through this?*

When we reach the bitter waters of life, that is when we are tested in everything we know about God and ourselves. Right amid our own trials, while we are asking God our questions, He is asking us a few questions as well, such as: *Who am I, beloved? Do you believe My promises? Is there anything too hard for Me? Do you trust Me to be with you always? When will you surrender your all to Me? Where will you choose to live in eternity? Why do you keep looking back from whence I delivered you? Do you love Me with all of your heart, soul, mind, and strength?*

Did you know that every question--ours to God, and God's questions to us--are all found in the scriptures? This is crucial to know, believe, and understand as we endure life each day as followers of Jesus Christ.

Jesus taught His disciples that in this world there will be trouble. In other words, things will not always be serene and jolly. We will not always feel like queens on top, diamonds, God's chosen, or even that we are saved by grace. The good news is that Jesus says that in Him we might have peace. He instructs us to be of good cheer because He has overcome the world. That is a powerful statement to ponder over and receive in our hearts when we face trouble. We must decide to not allow emotions to lead us during our troubles but to live life as a high-powered warrior. We fight strategically, with power and a plan!

It's Time to Stand and Fight!

Put on the whole armor of God, that ye may
be able to stand against the wiles of the devil.

--Ephesians 6:11

As women, many of us love to get dressed. I see you all, my sisters. You are fabulous. And even my young sisters, they can make a sweatsuit and sneakers look sharp these days. We love to get dressed in what makes us happy.

I recall watching my mother get dressed up when I was a young girl. Her dress flowed. Her stockings had designs going down the back of her legs, and a silk bow that sat right above the heel of her cute high-heels. She topped it all off with jewelry, her faux mink stole, and sometimes a fancy hat.

I, too, loved to dress up on Sunday mornings, and even today I love to dress up from head to toe. I used to focus so much of my energy, time, and money on what I was going to wear. I would even get stressed out about it. Every week I sat in my sister's hair salon for hours to ensure my hair was slayed. But none of my fancy clothes, six-inch heels, flashy jewelry, stunning hairdo or made-up face could sustain me during the trials, pains, and calamities of life. Neither can these things protect me from the attacks of the enemy, Satan. In this Christian life, we battle against the powerful evil forces of fallen angels headed by Satan who is bitter, jealous, prideful, vicious, evil and wicked and whose goal is to steal, kill, and destroy God's chosen people. Let me tell you, the devil has an agenda and a plan and it's not to make you great in life.

When we are dressed up in our fancy clothes, accessorized with bling, an expensive bag, and fabulous shoes, we stand out, gain attention, and then become a target for a thief who believes we have something valuable that he wants. The same is true when we are dressed up in God: we catch the attention of the enemy simply because of our faith in Jesus Christ as our Lord and Savior. Satan sees your walk of faith, hears your prayers, and observes the love and forgiveness you give to others. The effectiveness of your spiritual gifts is evident in your everyday living. As a high-powered woman, you are accomplishing goals for the Kingdom and standing out as you stand on the promises of God.

Without a shadow of a doubt, you are a target for the enemy who is a thief planning to steal everything you have in God. Not because he wants what you have, but because he desperately wants to destroy the foundation of the relationship you have with God, which is faith in Jesus Christ. If he can convince you simply to not believe God, your life will be subject to his schemes. He knows this is what will give him power over your life. Will you quit on God when you feel like your world is crumbling or will you stand up and fight?

Let me share one of many stories. There was a time in my life when I was stronger and much more established in my relationship with God. I was preaching, teaching, and all was well in my neck of the woods. Unexpectedly, my son and I went through a dispute and I was estranged from my firstborn child. This was a major blow to my heart because we always got along well. He was now an adult and lived miles away in another state. This situation hit my heart differently and did not look like other problems I had faced with my children. This gut-wrenching experience provoked feelings of bewilderment. I was deeply hurt and began obsessing daily on what I could have done better or differently as a mother. I began to feel as though I had failed as a mother. My thoughts and emotions were driving me each day. Throughout this tumultuous experience, I was up late at night, unable to sleep, and crying almost daily. It seemed like the more I prayed, the worse things got. I was crossing all kinds of boundaries and interfering in my son's life.

Now, I will say this: mothers do have discernment, and it doesn't matter how far away our children are; we know when something is not right. I know you can agree. The Lord will wake us up during sleep, speak to us, show us in dreams, etc. anything concerning our children and we will immediately move into action. But I learned through this experience with my son that insight does not give us permission to act as God. Rather, this insight is an alert for us to pray, seek God's wisdom, be still, wait, and listen for direction from God.

After being in this season of estrangement for almost a year, the Lord told me to "let go." You know how it is as parents: some of us have a tendency to be "helicopter parents," hovering over our adult children's lives, ready to drop in and save them and respond to their every whim. Some parents never say no. Some parents try to control their childrens' lives, criticizing their every decision, being worrywarts and unable to focus on anything but worst-case scenarios. The truth is we love our children so much and become driven by fear of the inevitable. Behavior like this proves that we are not operating from a sound mind.

It is important to observe what we are doing when dealing with our children. Are we helping or hurting? Assisting or controlling? We must determine when to step back, let go and let God. When God told me to "let go," He meant that I needed to let go of control and to surrender my fears, insecurities, and desires to Him. I needed to take several seats and give my son his space and the opportunity to hear from God as well. When we let go like this, we are not letting our children go in our hearts but admitting that some things are out of our reach. We must remember that we serve a God who knows all, sees all, and is able to fix it all. Without realizing it, I had allowed this estrangement to become an idol in my life, so I suffered and lacked peace through this unpleasant experience.

One evening, I was trying to read the Bible and hoping to find peace. Instead, I allowed my negative thoughts regarding my son to get the best of me. I asked God how could this be? I started bargaining with Him by going through my good-Christian-girl list: "I am preaching and teaching, trying to be obedient to Your Word, praying for others and helping families, but I am unable to help my own." I told God I was going to step down and quit ministry. I was frustrated, upset, and felt helpless. I was grieving the death of the relationship with my son. My husband came downstairs and urged me to come to bed. I told him I would be up soon, only to stay up in despair. That night, I closed my bible at one in the morning, told God I was quitting, and went to sleep.

My alarm went off at 5:00 a.m. Now, at that point in my life I had been having dates with God every morning for quite some time. But that morning, I told myself I was not meeting with God. Then something happened. I went to the bathroom and from the corner of my eye, I saw a book I had in a bin on the floor titled *Holy Spirit* by Charles Spurgeon. It was like God magnified the title of this small book to get my attention. I could not resist the urge to pick it up. I opened it and before I could read anything inside, the Lord boldly spoke these words from Matthew 10:37-38 to my heart: "Anyone who loves their father or mother more than me is not worthy of me; anyone who loves their son or daughter more than me is not worthy of me. Whoever does not take up their cross and follow me is not worthy of me."

I was immediately convicted. I saw how I had made all the challenges in my entire life all about me. I even allowed this estrangement to be all about me and my pain. I failed to listen to God who would be the answer to bringing my family and me through this situation with power. I was not fighting this battle like a warrior. You see, a warrior is a *brave* and *experienced* soldier who believes they will win the battle and thus win the war. The warrior should always operate from a victorious mindset. I was obsessed with winning but fought the wrong way and was only losing. I did not employ the strategy of the commander, who is God, when dealing with this battle. Although I was praying, I lacked faith and did not exercise wisdom. But the scripture from Matthew pricked my heart and opened my spiritual eyes to see how I must not allow the disparities of life to convince me that God is not who He said He is. I must take up my cross and follow Him.

I learned that there are some things I cannot control. I learned that warfare is real and that being armed with my spiritual weapons and trained in how to use them is fundamental in my spiritual walk with the Lord.

Shortly after this revelation from God, while I was at work, a dear friend who had been a confidante during this time quoted a scripture to me that I had never heard before. That evening as I read the scripture and talked to God about what she had said, God whispered to me: "I am making you into a warrior." At that very moment I broke into a praise and felt a divine move of God in my spirit. I was ready to fight the right way. I totally snapped out of my sappiness, sadness, and hopelessness. Whatever you are going through, my sister, God is making you into a warrior!

I then put a strategy for warfare in place. I began searching the scriptures that pertained to my situation. I started imagining the outcome I desired in my heart. I spoke life to my situation every day. I started praying with power and declaring the Word of God. I believed God was able and that whatever the outcome was, I would trust Him. I fully surrendered it all to God. I wrote bold and confident prayers of faith in my journal.

Within about eight months, God unexpectedly turned the entire situation around. It was a miracle and God did it. My son and I reunited and are now closer than ever. He is successful, loving, an awesome father, and has been a complete blessing and joy to our family.

My son and I look back now, laugh, and thank God for all He has done. I learned so much through this particular experience about spiritual warfare, idols, sin, pride, faith, and how to be a strategic warrior! The scriptures teach us that we are more than conquerors, overcomers, and victorious in Jesus Christ: we have the victory because of the finished work on the Cross. When we say we have the victory, we are not just speaking words that sound good; we speak the truth, and beginning with a victorious mindset is the key to believing in that truth as well as living a victorious lifestyle.

The Whole Armor of God

Ephesians 6:12 warns that there is a struggle with spiritual forces of evil in this world, not a struggle with flesh and blood. When we understand and accept that the struggle is real, we are better prepared when it comes. I believe the warfare strategy in Ephesians 6 is one of the most important passages in the Bible. We are facing battles every day in the world where we live. The worst thing a soldier can do is show up to a battle inexperienced, unprepared, weak, and afraid. We must be ready for warfare. It is crucial to understand that the struggle will continue throughout our journey until Christ returns. If we don't embrace this reality, we will easily find ourselves entangled in destructive situations resulting from the bamboozling trickery of the evil one, who desires to sift us like wheat. He will attempt to disrupt your life every chance he gets.

Do you have on the entire armor of God? There are six necessary pieces of armor to have on according to Ephesians 6:10-17. Each piece is necessary for spiritual warfare. We will need the armor against the evil schemes of Satan and in the evil day. Guess what? The evil day is now. There is surely evil happening now in our world and in seasons of our lives.

The *first* piece of armor is the *belt of truth*. The truth is the foundation on which we stand. Jesus declares in John 14:6: "I am the way, the truth, and the life, no man cometh to the father but by me." Every piece of armor is connected to Jesus. He is the Truth, and the Truth has made us free. The Bible describes Satan as the Father of Lies. He will spew out lies, accusations, and threats like a machine gun, which will make you want to run, hide, retreat, and surrender. Satan will tempt us in the slickest and most manipulative way to doubt God. He will create chaos and then ask you, "Where is your God now?"

Do you know the truth? The truth of Christ exposes darkness.

The *second* piece of armor is the *breastplate of righteousness*. Through Jesus we are the righteousness of God, meaning we are in right standing with God through our faith in Christ. Our faith gives us access to the goodness of God as we are accepted and approved by Him. The breastplate of righteousness will guard our hearts and protect us from being deceived. When we are in right standing with God, we are empowered to do good and live honorably. Proverbs 4:23 says, "Above all else, guard your heart, for everything you do flows from it." We will be tempted to do wrong, but we put on the breastplate of righteousness and obey God as we walk with Him.

The *third* piece of armor is the *shoes of the gospel of peace*. Through Jesus Christ, we have peace with God. We are not enemies with Him.

We also have peace with one another. With the knowledge we possess about our Lord, we are able to go forth and proclaim the good news about Jesus and the true peace that is available through Him. The shoes of peace are priceless shoes, and they are blessed and favored by God. When we put on the shoes of peace, we are motivated to go forth with vigilance spreading the good news. We will be firm-footed and hold our ground when attacks come.

The *fourth* piece of armor is the *shield of faith*. Our faith acts as a shield to protect us and intercept attacks. Our faith is a barrier against Satan's ambush that can cause us to doubt or not believe God. Without faith it is impossible to please God, according to the scriptures. Luke 1:45 says, "Blessed is she who has believed that the Lord would fulfill His promises to her." This blessing was given to Mary, the Mother of Jesus because she believed everything the angel of the Lord spoke to her. She brought forth the promised Jesus Christ. Our faith will shield us from the fiery darts of Satan and we will be able to stand anchored in God's promises. We are blessed when we believe even when we can't see the outcome. When the fiery darts come, hold up your shield of faith. Don't trip; trust God!

The *fifth* piece of armor is the *helmet of salvation*. I am going to spend a little more time discussing this piece of armor because Satan is coming for your mind. I hope your helmet is on tight. You will need every piece of armor fighting with you here. If your mind goes, then you cannot function. Salvation is the assurance we have in God and is an unbeatable defense against the enemy. First John 3:8 says that the son of God was manifested that He might destroy the works of the devil. Ephesians 2:8 says that by grace we are saved by faith. We have confidence in Jesus Christ's crucifixion, the blood He shed for our sins, and the resurrection of His body. Yes, Satan was defeated over 2,000 years ago! Always remember why and how you are saved through God's great plan of salvation. Read Romans 10:9-10 for the road to salvation if you are not sure.

Beware! Satan is on the prowl and he is coming after your mind to convince you that you are not saved. He wants to influence hatred in your heart for God so that you will ultimately denounce Jesus as your Lord and Savior. Second Corinthians 10:4:5 says:

"For the weapons of our warfare *are* not carnal but mighty in God for pulling down strongholds, casting down arguments and every high thing that exalts itself against the knowledge of God, bringing every thought into captivity to the obedience of Christ."

It is vitally important that strongholds and arguments that go on in our minds are brought into captivity, meaning that we need to bring them under control. Now, I know we have thousands of thoughts a day and cannot possibly capture every one. However, imagine a war fought between two groups of enemies. If the one group captures an enemy from the other group, they most likely will hold him prisoner. While in captivity, the prisoner will be asked questions such as: *Who are you? Who sent you? Who is your commander?* The interrogation process will be intense.

This is how we must be with our thoughts. It's time to do some interrogating. We must get to the root of what we are thinking and understand how our thoughts are impacting our emotions, behaviors, and overall lives. Either we can control our thoughts or our thoughts will control us.

Have you ever made a bad decision and asked yourself, "What were you thinking?" It's time to ask ourselves important questions before we make decisions that will impact us significantly: *Are my thoughts aligning with God's word, His Way, His Will? Do my thoughts push me further into pain, shame, guilt, sadness, worry, jealousy, critical judgement, condemnation, etc.? Are my emotions driving my behavior? What is this emotion I am feeling and why am I feeling it?*

The interrogation process is being mindful, aware of, and taking authority over your thoughts. By making a mental effort to think about what you are thinking and acknowledge what you are feeling, you will gain more clarity and be able to make your thoughts line up with the word of God with the help of the Holy Spirit. When you do that, the enemy loses every time.

The *sixth* piece of armor is the *sword of the spirit which is the Word of God*. Satan is a vicious fighter, and the Word of God is a weapon of destruction and offense. The Bible says, "For the word of God is living, and powerful, and sharper than any two-edge sword, piercing even to the division of soul and spirit, and of joints and marrow, and is a discerner of the thoughts and intents of the heart." The word of God is alive, and we never need to retreat when we use this weapon. We can fight the enemy head-on with the power of the Word.

I am big on spreading the importance of the scriptures. We must know them, read, study, and meditate on them. The Word of God is the absolute authority and works amazing power in the life of a believer.

Finally, the scripture encourages us to use *prayer* as a weapon. Prayer is calling in for backup on the battlefield. It is our strength when we are weary and more. The Bible instructs us to pray without ceasing, for all things, for all people, and believe for what we ask in prayer. Jesus told His disciples in Matthew 26:41 to "watch and pray so that you will not fall into temptation. The spirit is willing, but the flesh is weak." It is important to be aware of what is happening in our hearts, how we are thinking, and what is happening around us. Prayer helps us in all matters. God hears our prayers and will help us.

Our lives are valuable to God and He gave us important strategies that are rich in every believer's life. Who can stand against God? Who can defeat Him? To fight takes courage! One must be clear on what they are fighting for and have a made-up mind that it is worth the fight. It is a willingness to stand in front of danger, confront our fears with the truth, and have courage to not take the easy way out but stand in righteousness by faith declaring God's word.

For us to walk as high-powered warriors, we must engage in using the spiritual weapons gifted to us. Remember, resilience, character, and hope are built through our sufferings, losses, adversity, and sorrows. You are indeed victorious and a high-powered woman who is relentless, strategic, and courageous. Even on your worst day, you are still winning. It is never in our own strength or cognitive abilities that we win, but with the power of the Holy Spirit that dwells within us! We are not physically fighting. Our weapons are doing all of the work and the power of the Holy Spirit within us is helping us to stand!

Therefore, stand, high-powered Warrior!

Chapter 7
A High-Powered Wait

The long haul as a high-powered woman can be laborious, tiresome, and make you feel like your efforts are futile. Even waiting on something to happen can be worrisome: *Wait? Really? When will I arrive? When is it my turn? When will it happen for me? Are you telling me to stay where I am with a hopeful-expectation-while-looking-to-the-hills-from-whence-cometh-my-help kind of wait? The be-still-and-know-that-I-am-God kind of wait?* Well, my sister, the answer is yes. I would not have believed that waiting on God was the best thing until I trusted and tried it for myself. Yes, I suffered through waiting, and assuredly grew while in it. Psalm 27:14 says, "Wait on the Lord: be of good courage, and he shall strengthen thine heart: Wait I say on the Lord." My sister, there is a power that is manifested through waiting on God, and we must be sure not to compromise or quit in the process of waiting.

I must admit that impatience was my middle name. I did not want to wait. I was very impulsive. I was the kind of girl who would not think twice about dropping out of something or simply giving up on life, dreams, hopes, relationships, and anything else you could think of. I was often hasty in my behavior. I would make decisions swiftly without fully going through the process of evaluating the circumstance, weighing the pros and cons, or talking it out. I failed to consider the possibilities or consequences. I moved so fast that conviction didn't have time to set in until after the fact. Lowering standards and expectations for myself and others was a common practice. After waiting too long, I would simply give in or give up altogether. Things just seemed impossible to obtain and the difficulty of maintaining my standards was due to my impatience. Especially when it came to waiting on a mate to love me. I was restless. I ended up settling for substandard treatment and behavior that was unsatisfactory. I did not have the patience to simply be alone simmering in my singleness until the right partner came along. Nope, I would compromise my character, integrity, and my values. Over time my values were buried under layers and layers of fear of rejection, disappointment, and doubt, all as a result of impatience. Waiting was just not my thing and although I didn't show it, I would burn with frustration within, needing to make a move. On any given day, I would jump out of line, after shopping for an hour, in the grocery store. I would leave my items behind if I felt like the cashier was taking too long or if the line was not moving fast enough. I know someone can relate to this.

Did I mention road rage? I would have furious arguments with others on the road as if they could hear me and continued to fuss long after the incident occurred. I even had the nerve to tailgate or even try to pull up to the side of the other car and glare at the driver. But one day that all changed for me when I found myself on the other side of road rage.

One evening after work, dressed in my cute suit and high heels, I was driving to the mall with my two children, who were around twelve and five at the time. As we got closer to the mall, I noticed a car riding the back of my car very closely. As I turned into the mall area, the car made an aggressive turn and remained close to mine. I was not sure if this person was following me, so I made a quick right and then a sharp left turn to park near the entrance to the mall. It was now evident that I was being followed: with every quick move I made, the other person was on me like bees on honey. As I parked, I looked in my rearview mirror and saw the car blocking me in. Oh no they didn't! In a rage, I put my car in park, opened the door and jumped out without even thinking of the worst thing that could happen.

I headed towards the car behind my Ford Expedition. Inside was a petite woman much older than I, screaming at the top of her lungs through the rolled-down window that I cut her off. She then went off at me, cursing and yelling racist remarks.. With my children inside my car, the keys still in the ignition, and the engine running, I leaned into this woman's open window with my fist nearing her face. I had every intention of hitting her before I suddenly thought, *"What if there are cameras? And what if I hurt her and go to jail? And what about my children?* So instead of hitting her, I just exclaimed ,"OOOOOOOOHHHH." With a look of terror on her face, she sped off, still screaming obscenities. I stood there in disbelief for a few moments, replaying in my head that I had almost punched a woman who was about twenty-five years my senior. I gathered myself and I went back to the car. My son asked what happened. I vented to him and admitted that I almost hit this woman but that the thought of the possible consequences stopped me. Something clicked in my mind after I realized how this day could have had a totally different outcome. I was instantly delivered from road rage.

Sometimes things will happen in our life so that God can get our attention. I shared this story because this incident was not the first time I reacted this way. As God prepares us for different assignments or even our prayer requests, He takes us through a purging process, a growth process, and matures us. It is important that we mature in the process of growing.

My response that day at the mall was not mature at all. Why couldn't I just walk away? Well, there were some contributing factors: I immediately went into defense mode. This time, I was not the one riding someone's bumper, yelling or threatening but, the one being followed, yelled at, and threatened. This incident needed to happen so that God could show me myself. He revealed some deeper issues I had going on that influenced my anger and impatience: displaced anger, stress, control issues, fear, anxiety, and frustration. These mixed emotions kept me on edge and whenever I felt boxed in, threatened, or controlled, I reacted intensely. You see, years ago after I was in an abusive relationship, I made a vow to never allow someone to control me or make me feel afraid of them. I promised myself that I would never allow anyone to put their hands on me ever again without making them feel my wrath. I justified my actions as a defense mechanism.

What happened that day in the parking lot was not an aggression that just came out of nowhere; it was brooding within me and would turn me into a monster of a woman at any moment. Simply put, I could become unhinged at any time.

You know, I saw myself in that woman who had road rage towards me. Although I had lived so much of my life being out of control, I created a mindset that gave me the illusion of selective control. Yup, I thought. I would always be in control. When we operate from our perspectives that do not align with God's truth, we can easily make decisions from a place of fear, hurt, and anger. The truth is that healing was necessary for me here. I was making my own rules without fully understanding the residual impact of the weighty baggage I was carrying.

Waiting involves patience, and patience involves self-control, and self-control involves peace. Patience, self-control, and peace are three of the fruits of the Spirit named in Galatians 5. I must say, they work beautifully together. Now I am at a more peaceful place in my life and excited to share with you the power of the wait. Greater is always on the horizon when it comes to God. He has so much in store for us.

The Power of the Wait

Once I had a conversation with my brother, Levert, during my dating phase. This was after my divorce. I told him the struggle in finding a good man. He said something powerful to me that I will never forget: "Michelle, God has someone for you and is sending him to you, but you are all over the place and you are going to miss him. You are going here and there looking for someone and you need to be still and ready to receive who God is sending to you." I heard my brother loud and clear and often replayed those words in my mind and shared them with other women. They would prove to be true sooner than I thought.

After coming through a difficult year in 2009, in the beginning of 2010 I attended Sunday service at the same church where I hid in the back pew Sunday after Sunday. To my surprise, the First Lady was bringing the message. I remember getting excited to see her approach the podium. While I don't recall the sermon title, scriptural text, or the who, what, when, where, and how, I do remember her touching on the topic of sex and abstinence. I was shocked because I had never heard this topic come across the pulpit before. She also spoke about women knowing their worth. She told us women to not let ourselves be treated badly and then tossed aside like a rag doll tossed into a dumpster. That visual stirred my spirit as she spoke sternly, yet with compassion. Her words directly pounced upon my heart. I was that woman in the back who needed those exact words at that moment.

My heart was pricked, and the light dawned within my soul. I'm telling you, I came home with a new commitment to purity. I prayed to God and I promised Him that I would abstain from having sex until marriage. I wanted more, and I knew it would be through the complete surrender of everything to God, including my body. This journey would have intense challenges and setbacks along the way.

I started strong and was doing well on my new journey, but after some time trying to date and be abstinent, I gave in to temptation. I felt so guilty, worthless, and disappointed in myself. See how quickly guilt keeps showing up? But I had a desire to keep going and a determination that would not quit. This time, I had to really dig deep and remember how much God had preserved me over the years. I needed to walk this road the right way and with God's power. I went to God again, this time with a great plea for His help because the temptation was too great. I confessed to God that I broke my promise: *"Lord, I messed up. You preserved me all these years and I want to give myself back to You. This time I want to make a covenant with You that I will keep my body pure until marriage with the one You choose for me.* **If You will keep me, Lord. I want to be kept.***"*

If anything will mature you, waiting will. This time of abstinence and waiting to be married matured me. I had much more time for other things I previously ignored, like working through all that baggage I was carrying. When waiting on something, we tend to slow down. Perhaps it's the phone call you are waiting for, the mailman you don't want to miss, or the visitor who is on the way. When we are waiting, we are more still so that we don't miss a thing. That is a good thing. I was able to slow down worrying about finding a man for a while and work on me, my spiritual growth and personal development. I was determined to do this. It was more than abstinence from sex, it was training my mind and body to line up with the Word of God. I wanted to walk in holiness to see where it would take me. Holiness simply means being set apart, and that I was.

I stopped hanging out in places where I knew I would be tempted to backslide. My conversations were beginning to change. I started fasting, praying on my knees daily, and reading my Bible on a consistent basis. There is power in denying the flesh and what it wants. The discipline brings the mind and body into subjection with the Spirit. Although there is a serious struggle happening, the Holy Spirit is so powerful and works miraculously within us. If we make up our minds about honoring God, He will work miracles for us.

During this time, Patrice, who knew about this new season of my life, encouraged me to start attending classes at the Bible school she was going to. She told me about the transformation in her life as a result of the anointed teaching she was under. Immediately fear set in. I was afraid I would not grasp the teachings. There was so much I did not know about the Bible. Then, I received a call from the school inviting me to sit in on a couple of classes. I was curious and accepted the invitation. During my first day in class, I had no clue what the teacher was talking about, but I loved how she taught the Word, bringing it to life. I decided I wanted more, so I enrolled. My heart was ripe and ready to receive. I tell you, I was introduced to God in a way that I had never known. I fell in love with Him and had an insatiable appetite for His Word. The hunger was real, and my thirst was quenched week after week as I attended Bible classes.

Waiting is not just sitting passively, idle, or immobile; it's the necessary preparation to receive what you are waiting for. If you are waiting for your husband, it's wise to get your house in order literally, as well as your soul, body, and spirit. Start purging, growing, planning, living, and enjoying what God has for you right now. We miss so much of life, living for tomorrow, worrying about what may not ever happen or worrying about what could happen. We focus more than we should on tomorrow than on living on purpose each day.

Well, low and behold, I met a guy on the job who I had seen in passing for a few years but never interacted with. One day we had a conversation and things flourished from there. Brandon loved God, was brilliant, and hosted challenging conversations. We began to date and he was different from anyone I had ever dated. He shared his story of brokenness with me, his recent divorce, his children, and his season of surrender to God. He, too, was abstinent and in a place of healing and growth in the Lord. I told him about the Bible school I was attending, and he was so excited that he enrolled quickly. Our relationship with the Lord and one another grew.

During our dating period, we grew spiritually, continued to enrich our minds, and fell more in love. I must admit, I made it hard for him to get to me out of fear of possibly being hurt again. One day I had a dream about my deceased father that seemed so real. When I woke up that morning, I was overwhelmed with sadness and burst into tears because my father was not there. It was only a dream. I was so broken and realized how much I missed him. I went to the bathroom to cry some more and the Lord said to me, "No one is going to love you like you like your earthly father because that was a different kind of love. And no one is going to love you like your heavenly father." I immediately realized I was still holding on to my father in my heart and looking for my mate to be just like him. My father was the first male in my life to love me and believe in me. God spoke to me so gently at that moment and the fear of being hurt lifted. There was a release in my spirit that enabled me to completely love Brandon. He and I would talk for hours and hours and spent so much time together. My Lord, we struggled with temptation throughout our waiting period. We fought hard and there were times when we were seconds from giving in to temptation...but God! We were fueled by determination to stay committed to God and respect each other. We wanted to be examples for our children. I saw how Brandon valued me. I had never experienced it before in that way because I had never valued myself.

In 2013, Brandon proposed to me and on June 14, 2014 we joined together as husband and wife. And even now, I am smiling from ear to ear because I would surely do it all over again. Today, we understand the importance of waiting, the power in the wait, and how our marriage was united on a foundation of love for God first, each other, family, and others. I learned that it was our understanding of God's love that empowered us through and still empowers us today along with discipline and determination.

Prior to meeting my husband, I threw away my long list of requests because I trusted God to give me His very best. I only asked Him for three things: A best friend. Someone who would wait for me. And someone who loved God more than I did. God gave me everything I asked for and so much more. He did above and beyond what I could have ever imagined. Although no marriage is perfect, my Caramel King is unquestionably perfect for me and I say, "To God be the Glory!"

In the Waiting

Waiting does not have to be dreary or boring. While waiting, I learned so much about myself, others, life, and most importantly, God. Have you noticed the consistency in each chapter? Let me explain: everything we experience in life can draw us closer to God or push us further away. We can choose to see the best in every chapter and season of our lives as well as find meaning and purpose in all things. At times, it seems like God has left us sitting in the wilderness; but He hasn't. He is with us. God sees you through every toil and snare, pain and despair. He sees you. Psalm 37:4 says to "delight yourself in the Lord and he will give you the desires of your heart." Simply put, to delight means to bask in or take pleasure in something. We must pause from our busy schedules and bask in God's presence. For example, it's like going on a date with your mate and not talking about the kids, gossip, the news, neighbors, or church and instead telling your boo how you remember when he proposed, or your first date, or how he makes you feel, or how you enjoy the scent of his cologne. You will find yourself drawn into him more and him drawn more into you. It just happens naturally. You have now entered the intimate zone. You forget about the kids, bills, and everything else. It's just the two of you. It's the same with God: if we just bask in His presence without asking for a bill to be paid, a fine husband, to heal the sick, and bless our ministries, we will find ourselves simply delighting in Him. It springs us into a place with God, in His presence, and compels us to become intimate with Him on a deeper spiritual level.

Intimacy is powerful as it is a place of vulnerability, unveiling and exposing what is in the heart. To delight yourself in the Lord is to bask in everything perfect and true about God. You will be filled with unspeakable, overwhelming joy. This time with God is not the quick five-minute devotion and three-minute prayer that may typically start your day. This is a date with God. It is not to be rushed into or through. It is a peaceful pace, a pondering, and a patience that seeks out the deep things of God. This moment is freedom, connection, authenticity, and a drawing near to God that can lead you to the mountaintop to experience His Glory and be filled with His divine power.

To delight in God is to think about His grace and mercy, His goodness, His favor, His promises, His protection, His mighty works, and excellent greatness. It is impossible to leave His presence the same way you came. It is an opening of your heart and leaving all cares in his hands. Oh, then to continue basking some more in His truth, His righteousness, His wisdom, His redemption, and everything God has said about you as His masterpiece who is fearfully and wonderfully made. Oh yes, this delighting takes time without distractions and a busy schedule to just think about these things. Then can you imagine just being filled with adoration, gratitude, and thanksgiving? At this point, the tears are now flowing, and you know there is a God because you have never felt love like this before!

I can't tell you the times I have gotten lost in the delight of the Lord. I had to start a timer because the magnitude of the moment would capture every bit of me, and I would lose track of time. The more time we spend in the presence of God while waiting, the less impatient we become.

My sister, what are you waiting for? How are you waiting? Are you passively waiting or waiting with a plan? I would like to encourage you to do one of my high-powered disciplines that changed my life, and that is fasting. Fasting is denying yourself, for a period of time, while connecting spiritually with God. If we are honest with ourselves, many of us have idols in our lives that are taking the place of God. I shared in a previous chapter how I was making myself an idol. Everything was: *Why me? Why not me? What about me?* The discipline of fasting puts a halt to selfishness and vanity and puts the focus back on God. It puts things back into perspective.

Fasting is a weapon to use while you wait to help mortify the flesh and bring it into subjection and under God's control. Fasting was the turning point in my life, along with my desire to obey God, honor Him, and finally stand up to the mess in my life. Remember, your wait is personal. It does not have to be for a husband; it can be for anything you are desiring and expecting to see happen.

I must warn you that being obedient to God or fasting is not a bargaining tool to get Him to do what we want. Some people will do all these things and then say, "Hey, God, I fasted, I prayed, I obeyed; where's the promise?" God instructs us to do all of these things to bring us into alignment with His Will for us and into a new level of maturity. It also prepares us for when God says no even after you have waited for His yes.

High-powered woman, you can do all things through Christ who strengthens you! A high-powered wait is necessary, my sister, because greater things are waiting for you! God has not forgotten you!

Let patience have her perfect work, that ye may be perfect and entire, wanting nothing.--James 1:4

Chapter 8
A High-Powered SUCCESS

"Success is the achievement of the goal or purpose.
Live out your purpose--achieve success!"
--Michelle L. Primeaux

Achieving your God-given purpose during your lifetime is a success and a beautiful thing. God placed purpose in our hearts. Carrying it out becomes a passionate desire. When purpose is fulfilled, it produces upon the earth and brings the satisfaction of success. It is rewarding, provides a high level of peace, and can boost our spirits. You will most likely be inspired to do more and achieve even greater after experiencing any level of success.

I recall rather vividly reciting at the age of ten a passage from the book of Luke that told the story of Jesus's birth. This took place at my mother's annual Christmas Candlelight Service. My parents knew how terrified I was to speak in front of a small crowd let alone a huge one; nevertheless, that was my assignment. My father taught me how to memorize scripture and his excitement made the process fun. He had a way of turning your frown upside down and changing a boring time into a lively experience. I remember the first night of memorizing scripture my father called my mother who was in the kitchen and told her how great my memory was. Dad's praise boosted my confidence because I did not think I could retain that many verses. I remember how animated he was when reading the scripture to me. The inflections and how he enunciated each word kept my attention. I learned quickly and was ready. In fact, I still memorize scripture like that to this day.

The Candlelight Service finally arrived, and Mom dressed me up to look like Mary, the mother of Jesus. The church was packed, and I thought I was going to die. I was super nervous because although I knew I could recite those scriptures in my sleep, I feared people staring at me. I was nervous about forgetting everything I learned and I didn't want to embarrass myself and my parents.

Now it was my turn on the program. I stood in front of the church with the microphone stand before me. Surprisingly, I recited each verse without missing one word and the people jumped to their feet applauding. I remember the bright smiles and proud looks on their faces that made me feel approved of and relieved at the same time. I had achieved success in that moment by memorizing and reciting scriptures in front of a large audience without quitting or running away crying. I did it! My parents were proud, I felt good, and now I knew that learning scripture was one thing I could do well.

Success is a common word and defined by the *Merriam-Webster Dictionary* as the degree or measure of succeeding. Another definition for success is a favorable or desired outcome, as well as the attainment of wealth, favor, or eminence. If you look at the definition of success closely, you will see the word *measure*. Measuring something means looking at quantity, capacity, or the extent of that something. Society often measures success by the singular definition of wealth attainment, hard work, favor, or eminence. It places attention on how wealthy a person is and how competent they are at what they do. It magnifies how hard a person has worked to achieve success and how much education they have. Additionally, society considers one's connections, influence, and grandiose lifestyle. Because of this, society often shines a light on those who achieve these things, leaving others in the shadows of insignificance. Some believe that they have had successful moments, but not necessarily success overall.

When you hear the word *success*, do you see yourself? Although the word only has seven letters, it is a big deal. When some hear the word *success*, they may think *great*, *influential*, *gamechanger*, or *impactful*. Some desire success so greatly that they go all-in in chasing it. I must warn that if you start the journey to success without full understanding of what you really desire to achieve and how you're going to get there, the journey may present a greater struggle than necessary. I highly recommend having a strategy to reach your goal to keep you on course. Most importantly, seek God first in all things. Taking the time to be sure where you are going is wise and can prevent an unending cycle of burnout and unfulfillment from chasing success. Did you know that true success in the eyes of God is our faithfulness to Him in all our ways?

The Chase

The chase for success can be vicious as it can lead us down a path that is out of God's perfect will for our lives. There is a strong influence to be great that stems from things we have seen, heard, and dreamed about. The chase for success in life can be a concealed barrier to peace, contentment, and gratitude. We all have the tendency to seek after people, places, and things that appear to be greater than we are.

The daily chase after success in every area of my life was exhausting and I was just getting by each day on surface-level living. I'm sure you can agree that deep within, you have a desire for something greater. As a young child, I would play tag with the kids in my neighborhood. If you were "it," you would chase the other kids and tag as many as you could. I remember I chased one boy for a long time. I chased him down the hill, up the hill, around the parking lot, around the block, until I was so out of breath, I couldn't go any further. I was sweaty, frustrated, and felt like it was all pointless because I wasted my time going after him even though I knew he was faster. I quickly learned to chase the slower kids and tag them out before going after the faster kids. Then I enjoyed the game more and felt more accomplished in the end, even if I couldn't tag everyone out.

In life, we have a tendency to chase the idea of success, and for some of us, that is far beyond our reach. We begin the chase to gain more and more and find the years have passed by. We become tired, frustrated, and feel like we didn't gain anything from it. This can leave us feeling unfulfilled. The heavy weight of needing to prove we are a success can keep us pushing even harder, believing our time is running out. What was it all for? What are you doing with your life? Does what you do have meaning?

In the book of Ecclesiastes, King Solomon, whom scripture describes as the wisest and wealthiest King, states these words in his old age: "'Meaningless! Meaningless!" says the Teacher. "Utterly meaningless! Everything is meaningless!'" He then goes on to say: "What do people gain from all their labors at which they toil under the sun?"

Wow! I remember studying Ecclesiastes, and these words convicted me to stop, think, and ask myself, "What am I doing? Am I living a meaningless life or a meaningful life?" The next question I asked was "How am I living?" King Solomon talks about life being a vapor. This is true, as we watch the seconds, minutes, hours, and days disappear like mist. A vapor is here and then it is gone. You cannot grab hold of it. It cannot be stored up for later. Therefore, we need to focus on meaningful and impactful moments. Planning ahead is a good practice but some live in the future and never give full attention to the moment. Most people have a hard time replaying their week back because they cannot remember what they did each day. Do you know how you are spending your mornings, afternoons, evenings? Is everything a blur or are you mindful of how you spend your time? Is it productive or wasteful? Are you effective in your living or do you feel your living is in vain?

These questions are to initiate critical thinking that will inspire awareness that can lead to honesty and influence our action towards changed behavior. You don't want to have the attitude of King Solomon by believing your life is meaningless. Without an understanding of your actions each day, you may continue to find yourself chasing after the wind.

In the book of Jeremiah, God was angry with the people of Judah, His chosen people, because they were never satisfied with what He had blessed them with. They were repeatedly chasing after gods of other nations. God commanded that no other gods are put before him. He told the prophet, Jeremiah, to tell the people: "'Do not run until your feet are bare and your throat is dry.'" But you said, 'Oh, it's no use! I love foreign gods and I must go after them'" (Jeremiah 2:25). God had delivered the nation of Israel, fought for them, protected them, and provided for them in such great abundance. He promised them good things and that He would be their God and they would be His people. I love this scripture because it reminds me to slow down, stay focused, and to work smarter, not harder. I encourage you as well to take this time to evaluate your life and what you desire to succeed at. Is God the author of your plans? He is right there and has given you everything you need to live in prosperity and abundance without running your feet bare.

Grab a pair of your everyday shoes and check the soles to see how worn they are. Take a moment to pause and reflect. What are you doing in these shoes? Where are you going? Where does this path lead? How worn down are your shoes? Perhaps if your shoes are worn down, then it is possible that your physical body is feeling worn down as well, and so is your soul. For some, there is continuous running until their throat is dry, which can cause exhaustion and dehydration.

Every day, thousands of people are admitted to the hospital from being dehydrated. Many are running, pursuing, and chasing without stopping to hydrate. And then if we do hydrate, we are drinking the wrong thing. What are you drinking while reaching for success? Could it be....

- [ ] **Pepsi** of *perfection*?
- [ ] **Gatorade** of *greed*?
- [ ] **Sprite** of *spending addictively*?
- [ ] **Coffee** of *conformity*?
- [ ] Or the sweet **fruit juice** of *fear of not being satisfied*?

Jesus told the woman at the well in John 4:14, "Whoever drinks the water I give them will never thirst. Indeed, the water I give them will become in them a spring of water welling up to eternal life." Ah, how refreshing it is to be hydrated spiritually, no longer needing to chase society's version of achievements but working daily doing what God has created you to do. This will bring satisfaction and peace. You have spiritual gifts that are used to fulfill the plans God has for you. Work at removing the idols in your life: selfish ambitions, love of this world, fear, and lack of self-worth, all of which interfere and can place you on the wrong path. Recognize when you begin to compare yourself and your life to others', as well as when you look for validation from others to legitimize what God Himself already has.

Validation

There are many who struggle with embracing their personal successes in life because they do not believe they are enough and seek out others to validate them in a variety of ways. It is possible that after you have accomplished a goal, you can feel as though something is missing and look for others to tell you that you did a great job.

When I began doing ministry as a preacher and Bible teacher, I struggled with needing to be validated as a credible preacher and teacher. Although God had called me, I still struggled with believing I was worthy to have the title of a minister. I struggled with my confidence as I consistently compared my abilities, qualifications, and execution of my assignment with those of my counterparts in ministry who were more experienced. In addition, I did not fully understand why God had called me. But a flame of passion had ignited in me to study, understand, and share God's word and the gospel of Jesus Christ with others. In addition, I desired to empower, inspire, and challenge others to whole living after seeing what God had done in my life. My spirit was ready, but my flesh was fighting against it, and the fear of not measuring up and failing was making me sick.

Do you compare your achievements and overall life with those of others? Are you not reaching for success because you fear not being enough or good enough? First Thessalonians 5:24 says: "The one who called you is faithful, and He will do it." When God calls us to anything from motherhood to CEO, He will do it. If we rely on Him. When God calls us, He qualifies us, approves of us, and validates us even if no one else will. When I understood that, I began to move forward on everything God assigned me to do. I was still afraid on many occasions, but my faith in God and the working of the Holy Spirit produced a high-powered success.

My sister, believe that you are a success. The enemy will try to run interference, but your faith and determination to go for the goal will work for you. Be empowered by the one who called and validated you straight from the throne of heaven.

To know in the deep wells of your soul that your validation comes from God, brings a greater confidence and excitement when striving in life. My sister, God has created you in His image and likeness with the ability to create, be successful in good works, prosper, experience His glorious riches, and cause you to thrive according to His will. Believing this will end the cycle of comparison, needing to outdo another person, and seeing success as a reward of your obedience. It will also dismiss the need to be seen, heard, or recognized. Oh yes, high-powered woman, you will gain much more confidence and avoid the offense of being overlooked and feeling that you are not good enough, and begin to enjoy living out your assignments for God with power under His anointing.

The Ultimate Success

I want to share a story to encourage you on your journey and steps to ultimate success. I love being a long-distance runner. I have been running officially now for eight years. I started in March of 2013 after a coworker invited me to start a running journey with her. We used an app that trained us in sixty days to run five kilometers without stopping and we completed the training.

I learned to really enjoy running as my lungs and legs worked in sync. After I achieved that goal, I wanted to go further and faster, so I did, and I met that goal. I got even more excited and by July I was running seven miles without stopping. I registered for my first half-marathon that consisted of running 13.1 miles. I continued running about four days per week, going faster and completing nine-minute miles. By September, I was up to eight miles running until I began to feel sharp pains in my left knee. At one point, I was about a mile and a half from my home when the pain hit so hard that I had to limp all the way home with tears welling up in my eyes. I saw a sports doctor who took x-rays and could not find anything wrong. I was diagnosed with runner's knee and referred to a physical therapist.

On my first day there, the therapist had me do a series of exercises. After I completed them, he looked at me and said, "How were you running eight miles on a weak core?" He explained that the major muscles of the core section of our bodies are the belly, mid- and lower back. He told me that mine were very weak. He then explained that my sneakers were no good for my feet and for running long distances. I have something called *overpronation* from being flat-footed, which causes my ankles to roll inward with each step. This causes stress on the lower leg and can also cause knee pain.

This was astonishing to me. There I was, trying to be so fast and run so much without consulting a physician first! I had no knowledge, no training, or even the right equipment to be successful. I had to continue therapy for some time, purchase the right kind of sneakers, strengthen my body through weight training, and simply rest my knee from running. I was unable to run my first half marathon. However, I refused to quit, so I did everything I needed to do to restore my body and run again. In six months, I ran my first half marathon, an entire 13.1 miles, in the cold and pouring-down rain. I ran strong and felt good by the end of the race. My husband, Mommy, sister, and my daughter stood out in the rain as I ran for two hours and forty-five minutes. As I neared the finish line, I saw them all cheering me on and heard them scream my name. Even the race commentator loudly called my name and race number over the speaker right as I crossed over the finish line. Words could not express just how good that felt as the tears of victory mixed with raindrops cascaded down my face. I did it! Although it was a long, laborious, and painful journey at times, there was much I learned about myself. I kept pushing forward and refused to submit to defeat, setbacks, challenges, and pain.

Apostle Paul compares life to a race, and I understand why. I learned through the sport of running the seven fundamental keys to success are: commitment, consistency, focus, determination, discipline, training, and faith. I learned I would use these seven areas of success as I live a life of diligent service to God.

My sisters, there is a finish line where your reward awaits. See how far you've come and refuse to turn back. Stay diligent until the end.

Here are the seven fundamental areas of a high-powered success and the scriptures that have empowered me along my journey:

1. Commitment (Matthew 22:37-40): Be committed to God above all.

2. Consistency (Philippians 3:14): Keep pressing forward.

3. Focus (Hebrews 12:2): Stay focused on Jesus.

4. Determination (Hebrews 12:1): Run with perseverance.

5. Discipline (Hebrews 12:11): Discipline produces a fruitful harvest.

6. Training (2 Timothy 3:17): Be trained by the Word of God. It will preserve you.

7. Faith (Hebrews 11:1): Be fully assured in the hope. See the finish line.

Success for me is not simply about money or a lavish lifestyle. It is not about my name being recognized as the top successful person in the latest magazine. Although that is not a bad thing, it would be misleading to say I would not be happy if that happened. However, true success for me is knowing God, believing His Word, meditating on it day and night, following His commands, and carrying out each assignment that He has given me. Success is being wealthy in spirit, soul, and body. It is enjoying healthy relationships. Success is not running away from challenging goals but challenging yourself to win. Success is doing what you never thought you were capable of doing, not what others thought you could or could not do. Success is never proving you are capable; it's making an impact and being effective using every spiritual gift to the glory of God. Success is being authentically you, living life on purpose with a purpose, and enjoying the blessings that come with your faithfulness and obedience to God. Success is staying close to the heart of God, staying humble, and staying hungry. Again, success is working smarter, not harder, using wisdom, insight, and knowledge. Now that is a high-powered successful woman.

Do you see the fruits of your success? Every day you wake up, pray to God, and thank Him for His grace and mercy, take care of your family, go off to work, run the business, further your education, study something new, help others, and serve your community. I see you are doing it, my sister. Each day you are a caregiver for someone: scrubbing toilets, bussing tables, driving the school bus, driving for Uber, Door-Dashing, carpooling, writing the book, fearlessly running a board meeting, defending those who are the least and left out....the list goes on and on and on. Success is indeed achieved every day and your success cannot be duplicated.

My challenge to you is to create time to reflect as far back as you can remember and write out all your successes. What goals did you accomplish? What achievements did you meet? Put them in writing and then look at your list and thank God for every triumph and smile because you are a success story!

Embrace the ups and the downs, the wins and the losses, and definitely the joy that comes from it. There is a vibrancy to this life no matter what happens. Your attitude depends on how you experience joy through it all. It could be the feeling one may feel when they take a morning walk through the neighborhood and hear the birds chirping or a woodpecker pecking away at a tree. The sight of the beautifully embellished and brilliantly landscaped lawns. The joy one feels as they look to the sky and see the clouds placed perfectly. And if the wind doesn't blow or the sun forgets to shine, you know in your heart that you are okay. Success is even in the joy of strolling along the beach and looking at the ocean as the sun reflects crystals of light. It is in noticing the miraculous separation of the water from the dry land and realizing that only a brilliant God could create something so amazing.

Now look deeper into the ocean, as it appears so infinite in its existence and reflects an infinite God. Oh, the joy of a complete, balanced, courageous, and love-filled life, whether alone or surrounded by many. Eternal joy excites the hope of life and provides a fresh outlook on once-overlooked beautiful moments.

I now sing with King David in Psalm 16:11: "You make known to me the path of life; you will fill me with joy in your presence, with eternal pleasures at your right hand." Rest in contentment. Be confident in the fact that you are a success every day. Find your eternal happiness in God and spread the wealth because you are now one of the richest people in the world. You are a high-powered success!

Chapter 9
A High-Powered Love

Let love and faithfulness never leave you; bind them around
your neck, write them on the tablet of your heart. Then you
will win favor and a good name in the sight of God and man.

--Proverbs 3:3-4

Hate devours; love empowers! Some of the aspects of hate are insecurity,
fear, jealousy, pride, pain, and anger. Hate leads to destruction. But when
love enters the room, it overpowers hate with confidence, humility,
authority, joy, and peace. Love leads to restoration and empowerment.
When the sweet sound of the word *empower* catches the ear of a woman,
it can instantly inspire hope. The word *empower* means to give power
to. We understand according to the scriptures that God is love. We have
been given the power to love by God and He has called us to love one
another. I love what empowerment does for each of us. It keeps us united
in the center of God's will as we journey together on one accord.

However, many struggles within us can rise at any time and influence
us to operate from a place of hate instead of love. Anger, bitterness, and
hurt become an overgrown thorny bush around the heart, pricking and
preventing any entrance of true love, forgiveness, and peace.

Years ago, while on my knees crying out to God about an offense that caused excruciating pain to my soul, God spoke ever so gently these words to my spirit: "You are called to love the unlovable." At this time, about five months had passed since a relationship with someone close to me had ended. It broke my heart. I did not know how to handle my emotions as I was experiencing hurt from the deepest part of my soul. Some days I was so sad. Some days I felt betrayed and resentful, and anger would forcefully burst through. Each day I asked God to help me to get over it and to forgive because it hurt too much. But, the more I tried to, the more it seemed like the situation was growing uglier and uglier. I did not know how to handle the struggle, and what seemed so trivial to others was paramount for me. I could not see my way through.

If we live long enough, we will experience all kinds of hurt and pain from offense. This is a part of the world we live in. Offense comes in a variety of ways, through anyone, and at any time. I replayed the situation over and over in my head like a movie. I pointed out everything wrong this person had ever done and then beat myself up for not seeing the signs sooner. I asked why" and wanted it all to go away. But sitting on my heart were those same words the Lord had spoken to me: "I called you to love the unlovable." These are powerful words that in time I would surely understand. These same words are in line with Jesus' commandment spoken in Luke 10:27: "Love the Lord your God with all your heart and with all your soul and with all your strength and with all your mind" and, "Love your neighbor as yourself."

The truth of the matter was that I wanted justice. My faith in God and my confessed love for Him were being tested. John 2:4 says:" 'He who says, 'I know Him,' and does not keep His commandments, is a liar, and the truth is not in him." I was only keeping a part of the commandment, and that was loving God. But I was not loving my neighbor as myself. I was proclaiming my love for Christ but could not love my offender…

yes, I said *offender*. You see, I was offended and paralyzed at the place of my offense and was stuck. In addition, I became blinded by my pain and all associated with it. I really needed the other person to see just how wrong they were and how hurt I was. I hoped they would apologize and admit what they did wrong. I found myself telling my side of the story so others would feel sympathy for me and take my side. I wanted my offender to feel guilty and miserable at the same time. I didn't want them to have peace until they made things right. What I didn't understand then was that none of that mattered even if it came to pass because nothing can change what had already happened. The key was to check myself, humble myself, and just forgive. In exchange, God would be my comforter and healer as He promised in His word. I needed to embrace that this struggle was not against flesh and blood, but spiritual wickedness in high places. I needed to be renewed by the spirit of my mind. I needed every piece of my spiritual armor on as I managed life with this thorn in my side and the thoughts that were trying to overpower any good within me.

My heart began to change as I gained more understanding. Love grew exponentially within me and the peace of God flooded my soul regarding this situation. It took some time to get there, but I would not be writing this chapter if I had not gone through that monumental moment in my life. The greatest lesson I learned through this experience was discovering me. I saw who I truly was within. I was now fully aware that I was not so blameless in what had happened. I had offended the other person just as much as they had offended me. I had sinned and wronged not only this person, but many others throughout my lifetime.

As we experience trials in relationships, the fruit of those trials should be growth and maturity. To know oneself is to humble oneself. It was when my mindset changed that I began to pray differently. This resulted in my life changing for the better. The situation with my offender was tough because it had spread into almost every area of my life and impacted the connections I had with others. It grew wildly out of control. I felt so lost and alone during that time. God needed to do some more character building with me; I was not quite ready for how He wanted to use me. It wasn't about perfection; it was about readiness and effectiveness. I had to go through the refiner's fire for an intense purification of *my* heart. I had to know, believe, and receive God in my heart because He was love, and love was going to be a powerful part of my ministry. It was necessary that I learned how to forgive. If I did not learn the power of forgiveness, I could not be an effective and authentic minister, leader, and life coach today. God's love filled my heart towards this person, and even to this day, when I think about them, He shows me their gifts, the good memories I have of them, and the lessons I learned from our experience. Even when I remember the bad things, I can always see myself and smile because not only was I healed from that season of our lives but that person was too and so were those connected to us. Today, they are doing amazing things in this world. I am so proud of how we made it through. That's the power of God's love !

God's Love

Life is full of issues, lessons, and heartbreaks. But each experience is a learning opportunity as well as a stepping stool to elevate us to new levels on our journey. Early on in my career, I had a conversation with my big sister, Keisha, regarding the struggle I was having on the job. She was the perfect person to go to because she was a prayer warrior. I knew that she could pray for my situation to turn in my favor. Well, she listened and her response to me was:"Michelle, ask God to show you... you, and ask God for wisdom."

I was agitated at first by this response because I had poured out my heart concerning all the wrong this person was doing to me. This was not the response I expected. I wanted her to pray down fire from heaven on this person. I wanted her to pray with all of her might that God would put an end to this mess through some type of destruction. I wanted her to pray one of the prayers King David prayed when his enemies were on his back. I wanted revenge! We must be thankful that God doesn't answer every prayer with a yes.

I ended up taking my sister's advice and the prayer she taught me has been one of my prayers for over twenty years. Yup, I have been praying for God to show me myself and to give me wisdom. I often tell my sister, "Thank you!" That was some of the best advice she could have ever given me.

When we seek God from a place of humility, we gain clarity, His perspective on a situation, direction, and peace. Proverbs 4:7 says, "Wisdom is the principal thing; Therefore, get wisdom. And in all your getting, get understanding." Wisdom and understanding are key factors for us in giving and receiving love.

It is amazing, divine, and very freeing when we operate from a place of love. However, love must be understood, acted on, and given for us to receive its great rewards. God is love! He is the object, inspiration, and very source of love. As we are believers in Jesus Christ and filled with the Holy Spirit, we are a people who live a life of love. God did not give us permission to pick and choose who we want to love; He instructs us throughout the scriptures that we are to love even our enemies.

> Dear friends, let us love one another, for love comes
> from God. Everyone who loves has been born of
> God and knows God. Whoever does not love does not
> know God, because God is love.
>
> *-- 1 John 4:7-8*

Jesus, who was betrayed, arrested, falsely accused, mocked, maliciously attacked, and crucified, showed love amid hate. Right before Jesus died, surrounded by His enemies and wicked people, He cried out to God, "Forgive them for they know not what they do." Jesus understood the power of sin and had compassion on them. He became Grace that was the undeserving gift to all the world. It was the love for God that led Him to the cross. If we say we love God, then that same love will be overflowing in our everyday lives, even during persecution and hate. Love is a fruit of the spirit, and if we have the Holy Spirit working in us, then love will be produced in abundance.

Sometimes it can feel like you are all tapped out of love. You may feel like you have given so much love to others and that your love has either been rejected or abused. Most of us have experienced our hearts being broken repeatedly. It is important to take note that God is your creator and claims you as His own. When you take ownership of your love, you are making the decision of how you will distribute your love and to whom you choose to give it . That is why it is important to know that we cannot take ownership of the love we have because God is the author and creator of everything you see and do not see. We cannot choose who to love because we have been commanded to love all people.

As a new creation in Christ, your stony heart has been replaced with a heart of flesh and now carries God's love. As you are in God, His love can flow freely. God's love is pure, genuine, and able to be given over and over again. It does not run out as there is an overflow straight from the Holy Spirit Himself. This is confirmed in Romans 5:5: "And hope does not put us to shame, because God's love has been poured out into our hearts through the Holy Spirit, who has been given to us."

Love is so much more than a word; it has great power and impact and is eternal. Love has no end, no competition, and nothing can beat it. Sometimes in life, it seems like evil is winning, but the scriptures remind us that evil will have its day and love has already won. Satan will encourage thoughts that cause us to stay in a place of being offended, which will prevent us from being perfected by God. Remember the words in Colossians 3:14: "And above all these, put on love, which binds everything together in perfect harmony." Love is not being a coward. Love is a high-powered move!

As Romans 5 teaches, it is through our tribulations that perseverance, character, and hope are built surrounded by love. Allow love to dominate your feelings. When we know better, we should make a conscious effort to do better, as love, faith, and goodness will prosper us.

As we mature spiritually, we learn not to treat others the way they treat us; we treat them better under the guidelines of love. We are not doormats; we are high-powered women. We let God handle our lightweight and heavyweight issues. You see, God's love is not passive--it's bold and assertive. It is layered with discernment and wisdom and always defers to His lead. Check this out, sisters: the scriptures say that when the crowd tried to attack Jesus, He simply walked right past them and kept moving. We know when to shake the dust off our feet and move forward...all in love! When we experience God's love, we understand the divine nature of love, and we can love ourselves and others.

Loving You

Now that we have discussed how to be free in love and free from offense I have a few questions for you: How are you loving yourself? Have you taken the time to see the beauty in who you are? Do you smile when you think about yourself just as much as you think about your spouse, children, parents, or others in your life? How are you nourishing your soul? Beyond taking care of the outer you, how are you loving the masterpiece within? You are a phenomenal woman who is worth loving and being loved.

It is my prayer that you will take the time to nurture how you love yourself and see how God has lathered His love all over you. May you be empowered to live a life of love when you realize that it is *God's love over everything*. When you arrive at that place, you will: G. L. O. E differently.

G: God's
L: Love
O: Over
E: Everything

A high-powered woman has a unique G. L. O. E. She shines bright from within and attracts other high-powered sisters in her circle of influence. She models love because it is contagious and reflects true power.

Together, my sisters, we can surely do some damage to evil and hate. We can go get our sisters who are weighed down and help them go from brokenness to wholeness. Can you see it? Can you feel the hurt, jealousy, and fear oozing away from your heart because you embraced God's love that casts out all fear? Together, we can erase the stigma attached to the reputation that women have. Although everyone won't love, I believe there is a remnant of women who are ready and already loving! I am searching for high-powered women with hearts overflowing with the power of the Holy Spirit, faith, purpose, confidence, patience, peace, a warrior spirit, laughter, and adventure to join in and build God's Kingdom together in love!

Poem: Blowing Kisses to Heaven

Blowing kisses to heaven as my lips part to tell Jesus how much I love Him. I remember when I first felt His touch and heard Him call my name...my life has never been the same. But He reminded me that the first time I heard His voice call me, was not the first time He called me... it was just the first time I HEARD Him. So I blow kisses to heaven with a bowed-down heart in worship to Him who is my Lord and Savior...I blow kisses to heaven as I allow Him to take complete control. To take away all confusion, all worry, all pain...I blow kisses to heaven as I listen to Him whisper my name. My wretched soul cleansed and made whole, through the shed blood of Jesus who was mocked, beaten, and crucified yet, He arose. So I blow kisses to heaven and call upon His great name...Jesus...the name that makes me fall to my knees in awe, in reverence, in anticipation, in Love, in holiness, in truth...the name above all names through and through. I blow kisses to heaven thanking God for His Holy Spirit...my teacher, guide, counselor, wisdom and friend...He is amazing and I'm so glad we're together always with no end. I blow kisses to heaven for His angels that surround me, protect me, and cover me under their wings...I'm reminded not to fear, because heaven is always near. I am never alone as long as my God sits in sovereignty on His throne. I cannot contain His love, so I ask Him to enlarge my spiritual heart to receive more of Him. I love you, Lord, and blow kisses to you...more and more kisses. May you receive my kisses with all my love. Thank you for all the many kisses from you...the kiss of love, life, forgiveness, faithfulness, breath, purpose, strength, healing, peace, joy, and a crown of beauty...thank you for blowing kisses to me...I blow kisses to you. I love you!

--Michelle

Chapter 10
A High-Powered Queen

One day while returning home from Atlanta, Georgia, my husband and I met a man on the train as we were headed to the airport. He sat next to us but did not speak right away. After a few minutes, he spoke prophetically to my husband and asked him if he was a minister, to which my husband quickly replied, "Yes!" This prompted us to remove our sunglasses and look intently into the man's eyes. He encouraged us on our journey, and then said these powerful words: "When you are speaking, give them the dirt." He then looked me in my eyes and said, "When you look in the mirror you see your mother, don't you?" He said it so matter-of-factly and I responded, "Yes, I do." He didn't say anything else as he rose to get off at the next stop. My husband and I both looked at each other as tears welled up in our eyes. The two things he said that stood out in that moment were to "give them the dirt" and that I saw my mother when I looked in the mirror.

What my husband and I both believed this man was telling us was to give people the information that is not always fluffy, cute, and that caters to one's feelings. We are to give the good, the bad, and the ugly. But most importantly, we are to give the truth. When he spoke about my mother, it was so random and not connected to anything he was saying, but as I sat on the train and pondered that afternoon, I got it. It was the high-powered Queen he was referring to—something he hoped I would see and value.

I want to tell you a little about my Queen mother, as well as give you the dirt as you take your position as the High-powered Queen you are called to be.

I come from a line of phenomenal women. They are all beautiful Queens. These are women who are not listed in history books, do not wear crowns, and are not amongst the wealthiest according to society. I'm sure there are more people who do not know their names than those who do. However, I am intrigued by their wisdom, strength, confidence, resilience, and virtue. As far back as I can remember, my mother, grandmother, and great-grandmothers were classy women who I was blessed to know.

My mother, Sandra L. Todd, is an amazing woman who is the epitome of strength, tenacity, and grace, and who is a woman of virtue. Her faith in God has carried her and our family through tumultuous times and tragedies. She is God's blessing to our family and everyone who knows her. She is simply a woman who has pains, flaws, insecurities, fears, and struggles like anyone else; yet she is a woman who has walked intimately with God for many years. Because of her closeness to God, she is favored with wisdom and gifted with discernment. Her love is priceless, invaluable, and worth its weight in gold. Her love is rich and to be treasured. It flows deep from her soul as it fills the atmosphere wherever she goes. Her love is unforgettable. I learned so many lessons from my mother, and there are three I will share with you.

The *first* lesson I learned from my mother was that *loving beyond pain is possible*. Only my mother can share her story; however, through my eyes as her daughter, I have observed greatness. I watched the power of love and forgiveness work in my mother's life. She taught me early on to forgive and to never use the word *hate* when talking about someone. The way she would consistently love when she was hurt, give when she did not have, and listen when she probably wanted to speak was admirable. Her life was love on display. Mommy loved Daddy and took care of him in his sickness until he departed this life. Her sacrifice was unparalleled. I often ask God to help me be the wife who loves beyond. She had this kind of love because she loved God and followed His commandments. God's love empowered her in her weakest moments. Based on what I know about God's command to love and forgive, I see why she is full of so much joy and peace even in her latter years as a widow. At seventy-four, she glows as a radiant Queen.

The second lesson I learned was the *power of honesty*. My mother was a woman who did not want to lie and told us as children, "I can't stand a liar." When I was a young woman, she called me out countless times for being deceitful and encouraged me to be honest. On quite a few occasions by taking her advice about being honest I witnessed how I reaped a harvest of peace in my life through honesty instead of a harvest of destruction from a pattern of lies. The more honest I was, the more I experienced God's divine favor in unfavorable circumstances. I always tried to help God out by scamming my way into a favorable outcome--especially if I saw things going another way than what I expected. Constantly looking over your shoulder is nerve racking. But living authentically and truthfully creates an inward contentment. Your faith grows as you trust in God to work everything together for your good. Mom's commitment to honest living has yielded a harvest of blessings. Her life of desiring truth connected her to a life of faithfulness. Honesty coupled with faithfulness leads to abundance and trustworthiness in all areas of life. This bonds us with God and enhances our relationships. Witnessing my mother's friendships with other phenomenal women has been a joy. They have supported our family and been there for Mommy in the best and worst of times. This has been inspiring to watch. I love her girlfriends and enjoy seeing them stay connected over the years. You see, having longevity in friendships and sisterhood is based on a foundation of trust.

Finally, I learned how to be *a virtuous woman* of moral character, grace, gratitude, and a giving heart. When we were children, while riding in our family's car, my siblings and I laughed at a homeless person, and my mother was so upset. She scolded us and told us that man was someone's father, uncle, brother, or son. I never ever forgot those words. Mommy did not play when it came to talking negatively about someone's looks, weight, or if they were impoverished. To this day, I have such a compassionate heart for those who are without, considered as the least of them, overlooked, or abandoned. My parents valued all people. It did not matter what you looked like, where you were from, or what you had done, they understood and cared.

Another one of the beautiful memories of my mother is her kind heart. My parents did not have much money but my mother desired to give gifts to others. She would bake what seemed like a million cookies on Christmas Eve. I did not like to help in the kitchen unless there was baking going on. I loved to help bake the cookies so I could taste the batter and have the first pick of the burnt cookies that could not be given away.To this day, I love to bake. My mother would pack tin cans with the cookies and give them away as Christmas gifts. I later learned that a gift was never about its value, but the heart of the giver. The time, effort, and sacrifice for others was beyond priceless. It was love. My mother was indeed a virtuous woman behind closed doors. She was the spirit of the home, keeping it tidy and everything in check, including Daddy, my siblings and I...even the dog.

Mom was sweet as pie and stern as iron as she exercised loving discipline. She raised a family consisting of five children and had a husband who was her best friend. They were married for thirty-two years until death separated them. As a child, I surely did not agree with her strict rules and sternness. The word *no* flowed from her with ease when I asked to do things that were *not* in line with what should occur inside or outside of a Christian home. I could not stand it then, but I praise her today for being who she was. I praise God for blessing me with Sandra L. Todd. I continue to thank her relentlessly for her discipline and teachings as often as I can. She is a virtuous woman and her children arise and call her blessed.

My mother planted lovely four o'clock bushes right underneath the front window and they lined the yard beautifully. I remember the vibrant colors of the flowers that I would sometimes snap off at the stem and twirl in my fingers. My mother was an elegant woman of class, beauty, and wisdom. She was consistent in all her ways. She was fancy and always smelled good. She would leave the aroma of her favorite fragrance when she passed by and even her robe smelled sweet. She had a smile that gave life to a weak soul or a sad occasion. With her every stride, she exuded confidence yet humility, topped with a spirit of sunshine. I enjoy listening to her wisdom and talking to her on the phone for hours. I believe our longest telephone conversation was almost five hours--seriously. She is so easy to talk to and I always feel empowered by her. She is a high-powered Queen!

The Bible describes phenomenal Queens chosen by God to carry out assignments that would impact nations during their reign. The great Esther, who was full of courage and faith saved an entire nation from being destroyed. We also read about the Queen of Sheba who was a woman of wealth, wisdom, beauty, and power traveling an arduous journey just to seek wisdom and recognize the truth of God. I love the story of Queen Vashti as well. She was a woman of integrity and confidence despite the cost. Then Bathsheba, who was a woman of influence, just to name a few. To be a Queen was an honor, but not without enduring despair and even near-death experiences. However, these were royal women who were not perfect, yet demonstrated royal characteristics that we can all learn from.

The status of a Queen is a powerful one. First Peter 2:9 says that we as believers are a chosen generation, a royal priesthood, and a holy nation. This is by way of Jesus Christ and our faith in Him. John 1:12 says, "But to all who did receive him, who believed in his name, he gave the right to become the children of God." And if we are children of the King, my sisters, we are a part of the Kingdom of God and we have access and rights as Kingdom citizens. Romans 8:16-17 says, "The Spirit himself bears witness with our spirit that we are children of God, and if children, then heirs--heirs of God and fellow heirs with Christ, provided we suffer with him in order that we may also be glorified with him." With our royal inheritance we must know the power of our *position* as royal citizens and the authority that God has given us.

Around my mid twenties, I advanced into the role of a property manager. In this position, I supervised a small staff and managed a large property consisting of three hundred families. This was an intense position that required knowledge, skill, wisdom, order, confidence, and courage. In the beginning I was very timid and lacked the ability to lead authoritatively and gain control of the responsibilities of a property manager.

Fear played a major role in my inability to lead effectively. Additionally, I had to be told how to do my job rather than taking initiative based upon the power vested in me. I was in a position of authority yet I was operating as a subordinate with a novice mindset. I could not get the results the agency required and seemed destined to fail. I knew this was an excellent opportunity at my age and desperately wanted to succeed. I needed to press though, learn, and grow.

Over time, I learned so much and grew from a young girl to a woman and a successful property manager. I was finding my voice and learning how to use it. I was able to build connections and grow more confident in leading others. I often reflect on my years in that position, and I smile because those years helped to shape me, create a strong work ethic, and prepare me for a future in leadership. A key factor in that season of my life was maturity. Although I did mature a lot, I still had not fully developed and how I responded to pressure, opposition, and threats would cause my anxiety to surface and I would often have breakdowns and tantrums.

I discovered later that immaturity was one of my greatest downfalls during that time of my life. I have also found that immaturity is a real issue for so many. Immaturity threatens our position as Queens. It interferes with one's ability to operate from a position of spiritual authority, authenticity, and a Kingdom mindset. All of these are necessary to produce a character of integrity and a high-powered Queen.

Spiritual Authority

Authority is defined as ability, privilege, competency, liberty, power, right, and strength. As believers, we have the authority that God has given us.

There are two important areas of authority that we need to walk as Kingdom daughters. First, the ability to take authority over our own flesh. Proverbs 25:28 says, "Whoever has no rule over his own spirit is like a city broken down without walls." A person who has no control or command of their emotions or behaviors will be open to destruction as they have no restraint in place to guard against the enemy of our flesh--sin. God has delegated the authority we have so that we may do His will. Throughout scripture, God has not given a command that was impossible to carry out. God has delegated authority to us to follow His commands and provided the comfort, guidance, and power of the Holy Spirit. This empowers us to walk in authority. We have the authority to control the flesh, and if this exercise of power is not used, then you can be easy prey to the works of Satan. He will do everything in his power to steal, kill, and destroy. In Luke 10:19, Jesus said to his disciples, "I have given you authority to trample on snakes and scorpions and to overcome all the power of the enemy, nothing will harm you." As a woman with a royal status, you have been given authority, not of your own power but the divine power of God to reign. Be alert to the temptation to relinquish your rights through fear, disappointment, pain, and cowardice when backed into a corner by the adversities of life. You must know the authority God has given you over your flesh, and even the power over the enemy. Nothing will harm you even when evil has knocked on your door. It cannot destroy you because you have been promised a heaven and a home for eternity. And even now, this divine authority you have goes beyond your human understanding and is manifested in your life when you believe.

Kingdom Mindset

Doubt is not a part of a Kingdom mindset; you must believe. Jesus said to his disciple Thomas," You have seen and believed; blessed is the one who has not seen yet believed." To believe in Jesus is to be blessed.

As a high-powered Queen, you must have a Kingdom mindset because anything less than that will produce mediocre living. Having this mindset is to know God, who is the creator of the universe and everything in it, including all of humankind and every living thing. God is the Supreme being, perfect in power, wisdom, and goodness according to His word. He is almighty and a powerful ruler. God is the Master of all things, and no authority has been given to anyone or anything without His permission. Knowing God, His attributes, and His Word is everything when living as Kingdom-minded women of God.

"For this reason, since the day we heard about you, we have not stopped praying for you. We continually ask God to fill you with the knowledge of his will through all the wisdom and understanding that the Spirit gives, so that you may live a life worthy of the Lord and please him in every way: bearing fruit in every good work, growing in the knowledge of God." (Colossians 1:9-10)

High-powered Queen, it is important that we operate in a Kingdom mindset and not an immature mindset that becomes a disgrace to the name of God. We must be renewed by the spirit of our minds so that we will stand firm on the Word of God. Refuse to be wishy-washy or lukewarm with one foot in the Kingdom and one foot in the world. Having a heart for the things of God more than the things of this world will benefit our lives. We make the grand decision to refuse to be like the evil Queen Jezebel, who was insecure, messy, hateful, controlling, jealous, vindictive, and a murderer. This Jezebel spirit flourishes and shows up in homes, communities, on the job, and in the church. We must use discernment to evaluate our motives and the motives of others.

We must be wise women not easily swayed from the truth. We must walk in confidence and the certainty that the fight of faith is worth every blow, every knockdown, and every loss. A Kingdom mindset is knowing that for every loss, there is a gain. You will reign under the authority of God that empowers you to live a life worthy of the Lord who is your King and ruler. Resist the devil, stand up and fight, declare God's word in lifeless situations, and be biblically competent. You have the power and spiritual authority to manage your lives and households accordingly as you exude the character of a virtuous woman.

Integral Character

A respected character is rewarded with a rich existence in your royal position. A high-powered Queen refuses to forfeit her Kingdom reward by avoiding vices that will cause her to behave in unrighteous ways. She knows that righteousness illuminates her path and that others will follow this guiding light. There are some who use charm in leadership while deceiving others. Proverbs 31:30 says, "Charm is deceitful, and beauty is passing, but a woman who fears the Lord, she shall be praised." When a woman fears the Lord, she is praised because of her piety. Those who know her will speak well on her behalf.

A Queen refuses to disrespect herself by revealing the parts of her body that are sacred. She doesn't need to gain attention or influence by revealing what should be concealed. She uses wisdom to gain influence, not sensuality. How can we make an impact and earn respect if we don't show that we respect and value our bodies? My sisters, we must remember that classy is oh so attractive. We must carry ourselves as dignified women with confidence and pride. I see more nakedness amongst believers now more than ever. Don't kill the messenger; I must give you the dirt. Today's social norms have influenced women to look like what they see on television or in social media. Proverbs 11:22 says, "Like a gold ring in a pig's snout is a beautiful woman who shows no discretion." Our speech, our appearance, and our comportment should be attractive and not distasteful. Everything is not for us, every place is not for us, and everybody is not for us to follow. I appreciate my mother for calling me out on the revealing clothes I wore that only attracted attention from the wrong people. Queens are women of pride and power! That includes combing our hair and putting on respectful clothes when leaving our homes. We are representing God and our reputation.

I didn't always have a Kingdom mindset and was treated as such. The good news is that it is never too late to desire to grow and do better. We can watch other respected women and follow their lead. In Romans 12:1, we are urged to present our bodies as a living sacrifice, holy, and pleasing to God. This is your true and proper worship. *Always remember to value your morals. They protect your character and enhance your worth.* I remember another high-powered Queen telling me that I had "substance." She was right. I was useful, rich in the fruits of the spirit, valuable, and powerful. When we are tempted to damage our character, we must remind ourselves that we have substance. My sister, you have substance! Tell yourself this every day.

Our children see us and have impressive memories. We must change our thinking and behaviors so we can be examples for them as well. They are our legacy, our future, and we are raising Kings and Queens. The children of a virtuous woman will rise and call her blessed. Her mouth speaks wisdom, and she does not live a life of idleness or gossip. She lives a life of order and not chaos. She speaks kindness and not negativity. She values her worth and everything God has gifted her. She looks for the good when all kinds of bad surround her. She rises from the ashes with power and is not led astray by the venomous attacks of evildoers. Her self-respect shows in her outward behavior. She takes proper care of herself and her goal is to receive the crowns God has promised.

A high-powered Queen is a leader! She is confident in her abilities and not afraid to use them to impact the lives of others. She hears from God and is able to make wise decisions. She steps into her position of power knowing her birthright. The crown of beauty she wears replaces her crown of ashes. She is valiant and vigilant. She has accepted her position as a royal daughter and a servant. She brings her best to the table for others to dine on. She takes care of herself and surrounds herself with other powerful Queens who have the same Kingdom mindset.

You cannot do this alone. The high-powered Queen does not need to defend everything she does. She doesn't need to say yes to every request to prove she is loyal. She knows her limits and loves with boundaries, understanding that the word no does not mean she doesn't love or care. Her decisions are bold moves to expand and advance the Kingdom of God. She doesn't need to be seen, heard, or validated; however, her actions will surely go unnoticed. What she does privately, God will reward openly.

High-powered Queen, you are anointed, appointed by God, and laugh at the days to come. You are unique. Be serious about God and refuse to go back to where He has delivered you from. You are a high-powered Queen who is important and must know that YOU belong to God! Straighten your crown, my sister, hold your head up and be the Queen that you are! Your journey awaits.

Chapter 11
A High-Powered Journey

As we have come to the final chapter of this book, I am excited to see you embark on your journey, excel, finish the course, and continue making high-power moves unapologetically. I hope you are ready to go to new levels in your relationship with God, with others, and in your purpose. As you go, "Trust in the Lord with all your heart and lean not to your own understanding; in all your ways submit to him, and he will make your paths straight" (Proverbs 3:5-6).

The path is already laid out for you. Stay on the path of righteousness and continue to believe in miracles. God is able to do it for you. You are a miracle because all miracles provide evidence of the power and presence of God upon your life.

How are you a miracle? Take some time to do personal reflection and recall the miraculous demonstrations of God's power upon your life. This is your testimony. I guarantee, you have a story that confirms the miracle you are and the high-powered woman you are continuing to be. The Lord has taken you from brokenness to wholeness and that is a miracle. However, more awaits.

You made it this far; that means God still has more for you to do. God will perfect everything that concerns you. This is good news, because even for me, I still need much work and I still need to do work.

Enjoy learning new things about life, yourself, and God. May your eyes, ears, and heart be ready to hear, see, and do everything that God desires. Oh yes, the journey to this point has been one huge learning lesson for us all. But with the power of the Holy Spirit, you have been able to not only survive, but to overcome as more than a conqueror. This journey has afforded you so many opportunities to bounce back, grow, and gain understanding. Continue to live in hope, exercise your faith, elevate with courage, and develop a strong mind guided in wisdom.

High-powered woman, although this journey has not always been a day at the beach or relaxing by the fireplace, remember it is all working together for your good. Do not tear down the building blocks in your life because they are elevating you to new levels in God. Walk with your *high-powered Savior*, anchored in a *high-powered faith* in Christ, remembering your *high-powered redemption*, while walking tall in *high-powered confidence*, living out your *high-powered purpose* as a *high-powered warrior*. And don't stop there. Delight yourself in the Lord with a *high-powered wait* on God, being a *high-powered success* working smarter, not harder. Finally, have a *high-powered love* as you love the unlovable, and reign as a *high-powered Queen* through every season of your life.

Years ago, I was not equipped spiritually with the tools I needed to walk in power. I was saved but had no real relationship with God. I was reading books with no substance and not doing much to discover my high-powered status. I rarely spent time in prayer and worshiping God. So when life got hard, I yielded to it. I believed those hard times were characteristic of how my life would always be. Throughout life, we go through different seasons. Some are more difficult than others. This too shall pass. Ecclesiastes 3:1 reminds us of this. "To everything there is a season, a time for every purpose under heaven." Your individual season has a purpose and a time limit. I almost ended my life because of a very tough season. Whatever you do, never give up. Look for meaning in each day and find purpose in every season of your life. Remember, seasons do change. What season are you in? Are you in a season of birthing? Are you in a wilderness season? Are you in a season of grief?

Knowing what season you are in during the many stages of life is important so that you will understand how to nurture yourself and manage your seasons. You can be in a season of overflowing fullness right now. Your relationship with God may be nice and cozy, and relationships with others in your life may be thriving. Perhaps your finances are multiplying, your business is booming, and your ministry is growing. If this is the case, rejoice daily in the Lord, stay on track and focused and enjoy the abundance.

I have a question to ask you while in this season of abundance: How are you managing the overflow? This is important to monitor how you do this because you will need to be wise and a good steward because seasons do change. For example, the COVID-19 pandemic taught us a lot about how quickly this change can happen. The pandemic exposed many lifestyle deficiencies. As high-powered women, we cannot operate from deficits; we must properly steward the overflow.

A great example of this is the story of Joseph in the book of Genesis. God gave him wisdom in the season of plenty to store up for the season of lack, and as a result many were saved, including his family.

Many have lost so much because they did not prepare for when the season of lack came. I must admit that 2020 was a major wakeup call for me. The pandemic showed me there were things I had put off and needed to have in place. If we manage wisely, we will have an overflow as we move into the next season.

If you are in a dry season, what are you planting in this season to reap a harvest in the next? If you sow, you will surely reap in time.

Be encouraged if you are in a season of grief, loss, financial struggles, broken relationships, and weariness. Even in this season, you can sow seeds of greatness, choose to believe that you will endure till the end and reap a harvest of greater blessings." If you are in this season, I ask: How are you nurturing yourself in this season?" Also, what is your plan to get back on track?" Believe that the rain will come, the seeds sown will be watered, and you will receive all that God has for you. God's grace and mercies are real and powerful in your life. When storms of life come your way, don't run from them, but press through; you will make it.

I love this inspirational quote from Wintley Phipps: "It is in the quiet crucible of your personal, private sufferings that your noblest dreams are born, and God's greatest gifts are given in compensation for what you have been through."

The Merriam-Webster Dictionary provides three powerful definitions for the word crucible:

1. A vessel used for melting a substance that requires a high degree of heat.

2. A test.

3. A place or severe situation in which concentrated forces interact to cause or influence change or development.

A crucible locks in heat and turns it up to a high degree. While we are in a crucible, those hard areas within us are melted off as we are tested. God does a new thing in us as we go through the heat of life. As you come out of the crucible, you will be revealed as an authentic high-powered woman.

When I was around fifteen years old, my girlfriend and I took the train to Center City, Philadelphia, to go shopping. As we left the galleria, there was a man standing outside with gold herringbone necklaces in his hand. He saw us coming from a mile away. We were two naïve and unassuming young girls excited to be in the big city alone. He told us that his necklaces were 14-karat gold and they were only $20. We looked closely at them and saw that *14K* was engraved on their clasps. I quickly gave him the $20 and put the necklace on right away. You could not tell me anything, honey. But when I arrived home and told my father about my necklace, he laughed and told me that it was not real. I debated back and forth with him before he finally said, "Michelle, take off the necklace and I will prove that it is a fake." He grabbed the ammonia from under the kitchen sink and filled a bowl with it. I gave him my necklace and he placed it in the bowl. Within a few hours, the necklace turned green. I can't tell you how upset I was at my father. But the truth is, I purchased a fake necklace from a scammer knowing it was wrong in the first place and wasted my hard-earned money.

A fake person will be exposed when submerged in a hard place for some time. Authenticity is tested before it is approved and validated as genuine. It's a beautiful thing to be a woman and enjoy the fun girly things that enhance our beauty. But our outer appearance is not the main concern; it's what's underneath it all. To be legitimate as a high-powered woman, you have to stand the test of every season along your journey while holding to the truth of God. In 2020, my family experienced unexpected sickness and even worse, unexpected deaths that were devastating. Our faith was tested. It was faith in God's word and the power of the Holy Spirit at work in our hearts that gave everyone what they needed to live each day.

As we are in the crucible of life, we are tested. What we believe to be true and who we are at our core will be revealed. Second Timothy 2:20 says, "But in a great house there are not only vessels of gold and of silver, but also of wood and of earth, and some to honor and some to dishonor. If a man therefore purge himself from these, he shall be a vessel unto honor, sanctified, and meet for the master's use, and prepared unto every good work." In the crucible, when we go through the hottest temperature of our sufferings, God is with us. If we allow the purging to happen, we will emerge as a new creation and break forth with power.

My sisters, while going through the process of being transformed on this journey, ask God to help you to identify the barriers keeping you from being a high-powered woman. As it is written in Mark 7:21-23, "For it is from within, out of a person's heart, that evil thoughts come—sexual immorality, theft, murder, adultery, greed, malice, deceit, lewdness, envy, slander, arrogance and folly. All these evils come from inside and defile a person." As your soul submits to the power that is working in you, your flesh will come into alignment with the Will of God. Lift up your head and rejoice because you have the power to overcome anything. Remember your power!

IT IS TIME, high-powered woman! It is *YOUR* time! Come on, Queens. I pray that while reading this book, there has been a shift in your spirit that has loosened whatever was holding you back. Now is the time to break forth, depart, burst out of, and emerge. Come on out, my sister, into view and let's do a forward victory march. Be willing to leave the broken and destroyed pieces behind. Walk in your new season, with better opportunities, far greater than you could have imagined. God is all-powerful and His hand of favor is upon you. Break forth as a new creation into the more God has for you. This is just the beginning.

Let nothing distract you from your assignment that is the will of God for you. I can't say this enough. God's power that works in you cannot be stopped unless you give up. His power is uncontainable, uncontrollable, unstoppable, and imperishable. Additionally, God's power is undying, unfading, enduring, everlasting, and persistent. There are wonderful things available to you while on your journey. You have treasures and light in darkness, riches in impoverished situations, and a strong tower when you are weak.

"He will keep you firm until the end, so that you will be blameless on the day of our Lord Jesus Christ. God is faithful, who has called you into fellowship with his Son, Jesus Christ our Lord." (1 Corinthians 1:8)

The high power within will draw others to your Savior Jesus Christ as the Kingdom grows with more high-powered women who are fierce, fabulous, and forever God's beloved. A wise person once told me there is no finish without a start. In the words of Nelson Mandela, "It always seems impossible until it's done." Begin today! Go forth! There is nothing like a high-powered woman with the power of God, a purpose, and a plan! Proclaim today...I am a HIGH-POWERED WOMAN!

"I pray that out of his glorious riches he may strengthen you with power through his Spirit in your inner being, [17] so that Christ may dwell in your hearts through faith. And I pray that you, being rooted and established in love, [18] may have power, together with all the Lord's holy people, to grasp how wide and long and high and deep is the love of Christ, [19] and to know this love that surpasses knowledge—that you may be filled to the measure of all the fullness of God. Now to him who is able to do immeasurably more than all we ask or imagine, according to his power that is at work within us, [21] to him be glory in the church and in Christ Jesus throughout all generations, for ever and ever! Amen." (Ephesians 3:16-21)

Acknowledgements

I want to thank every woman who has helped to shape the high-powered woman I am today. From my childhood girlfriends to classmates, amazing coworkers over the years, the fabulous women in my family, mentors, ministers, teachers, and confidantes. We are all on our individual journeys, yet the same path to our destiny in God. We can't do it alone and are better as we go and grow together.

May we continue to link arms, strengthen, support, and empower one another to greatness. I enjoy seeing the beautiful flowers that bloom from the love and unity you all possess. I look forward to meeting and connecting with new high-powered women on my journey. I will have a huge smile and a big hug waiting for you. The high-powered woman is a movement! Let's do this!

I love you, my sisters, and pray God's very best upon you!

In love and faith,
--Michelle L. Primeaux

References

Scriptures: New International Version and New King James Version

Resources

National Suicide Prevention Hotline – 1-800-273-8255
National Domestic Violence Hotline – 1-800-799-SAFE (7233)

Contact the Author

Email Michelle Primeaux at thehighpoweredwoman@gmail.com
www.michellelprimeaux.com
Facebook: The High Powered Woman
Instagram: The High Powered Woman

CPSIA information can be obtained
at www.ICGtesting.com
Printed in the USA
BVHW032317301021
619987BV00006B/43/J